Learning Outside the Prim

'We believe that every young person should experience the world beyond the classroom as an essential part of learning and personal development, whatever their age, ability or circumstances. Learning outside the classroom is about raising achievement through an organised, powerful approach to learning in which direct experience is of prime importance.'

(*Learning Outside the Classroom Manifesto*)

In *Learning Outside the Primary Classroom* the educationalist and writer Fred Sedgwick explores in a practical way the many opportunities for intense learning that children and teachers can find outside the confines of the usual learning environment, the classroom.

This original work is based on tried and tested methods from UK primary schools. The author draws on current concerns in the educational world regarding outdoor learning, as exemplified by the eight-sector Learning Outside the Classroom (LOtC) initiative (supported by Ofsted), but remains refreshingly independent in approach.

Using a metaphor of concentric circles, *Learning Outside the Primary Classroom* starts with a brief opening chapter based in the classroom itself before moving outwards to explore the learning possibilities presented by the immediate environs of the school – playgrounds, gym halls, sports fields, etc. Later chapters move beyond the school gates to explore the local shops, parks, religious centres, libraries and town halls and the myriad learning opportunities they represent. The final chapters explore the possibilities of larger-scale day trips to major galleries and museums and more ambitious field trips.

Fred Sedgwick is a freelance lecturer, trainer and writer on children's writing, management, art, personal, social and moral education, as well as on Shakespeare and the young writer.

Learning Outside the Primary Classroom

Fred Sedgwick

Routledge
Taylor & Francis Group

LONDON AND NEW YORK

First published 2012
by Routledge
2 Park Square, Milton Park, Abingdon, Oxon OX14 4RN

Simultaneously published in the USA and Canada
by Routledge
711 Third Avenue, New York, NY 10017

Routledge is an imprint of the Taylor & Francis Group, an informa business

British Library Cataloguing in Publication Data
A catalogue record for this book is available from the British Library

Library of Congress Cataloging in Publication Data
Sedgwick, Fred.
Learning outside the primary classroom / Fred Sedgwick.
    pages cm
  1. Outdoor education—Great Britain.   2. Place-based education—
Great Britain.   3. Education, Elementary—Great Britain.   I. Title.
LB1047.S43 2011
371.3'840941—dc23

                                                                    2011045614

ISBN: 978–0–415–60866–4 (hbk)
ISBN: 978–0–415–60867–1 (pbk)
ISBN: 978–0–203–12034–7 (ebk)

Typeset in Aldine 401 BT
by RefineCatch Limited, Bungay, Suffolk

Printed and bound in Great Britain by
TJ International Ltd, Padstow, Cornwall

For Daniel, with love and gratitude

When My Ship Comes In

I never saw an ugly thing . . . old rotten planks,
slimy posts and brickwork, I love such things . . .
(John Constable)

Twice every twenty-four hours the moon
pulls into view my ship that has come in.

Drags water seaward. Exposes
wild wooden trapezoids of gunwales,

random planks pocked, green, diseased,
a dismantled dank ruined ship shape

at such peace. And there's a ladder
where a few decades ago a man

climbed upwards leaving my ship to die.

                        But I found it.
Woke it
            with a camera click
                        these lines.
                        (FS)

When you're out with children, wherever, on a day trip, a school journey, whatever it is, the authoritarian side diminishes, there's a companion thing you can't
have in the classroom . . .
(A teacher)

A photo of my 'ship' appears in Chapter 4, p 32.

Contents

List of illustrations   ix
Acknowledgements   x

Introduction   1

1   Writing and thinking   5
    1 Writing and making it better   5
    2 Really thinking   8

2   At home   9
    Getting writing out of the home experience   11

3   On the playground   21

4   In the town   31
    1 High street   31
    2 Football stadium   37
    3 The supermarket   40

5   Bringing something out of the earth   44
    1 An adventure in garbology   44
    2 The glow of the kiln in the woods   52

6   A day on Seaham Beach   57

7   In the gallery   69
    1 Making a gallery   69
    2 A Suffolk gallery   73

8   The Sainsbury Centre at the University of East Anglia   85

9   Where people worship   92
    1 Castle Acre Priory   92
    2 New every morning: a church   97

10 Two school journeys   100
    1 Drawing mushrooms over the sea wall   100
    2 From a school journey log   106

    Epilogue   111
    Booklist   114
    Index   116

Illustrations

My ship   32

The tepee in the forest   54

The figures in the forest   55

A poem from Seaham   60

Scallop by Maggi Hambling   75

Castle Acre Priory   93

Acknowledgements

I am grateful for the help I received from Duncan Allan, and for his letting me see project reports on Garbology and on Exploring Archaeology, on which I have drawn for Chapter 5.

I am grateful to teachers in the following schools who let me work with children outside their classrooms:

Aldwickbury Preparatory, Harpenden, especially Steve Lott
Central Primary, Newham
Middleton Primary, Suffolk
Sherburn Village and Hill Primaries, Durham, especially Teresa Leggatt
Sidegate Primary Ipswich, especially Jeannine Pearl
Springfield Junior, Ipswich, especially Michael Lynch.

I am grateful to the staff in the Learning Zone at West Ham United Football Club for their help.

I am especially grateful, as ever, to Daniel Sedgwick.

Poetry is present behind this book, mainly the influence of the works of T S Eliot, Thomas Hardy, Seamus Heaney, Gerard Manley Hopkins (he hated his middle name so I have dropped it in the text) and Philip Larkin. All their work is still in print and easy to locate. I have, however, given the volume details of the Heaney because there is no collected edition.

Introduction

> [E]very young person should experience the world beyond the classroom as an
> essential part of learning and personal development . . .
>   (*Learning Outside the Classroom Manifesto*, DfES Publications, 2006)

There is indeed such a world. And what the poet W H Auden calls somewhere 'our precious five' (seeing, hearing, tasting, smelling, feeling) tell us that we live every waking moment of our lives in it. Even here and now as I type on an early spring Saturday evening from the relatively sterile atmosphere of this room, I see dusk settle. The blue sky turns grey to the east and pale blue and reddish in a patch to the west; I can see (if I lean uncomfortably forward over my desk) the budding magnolia in my neighbours' garden. I can hear the traffic quieten, and the silence inside my flat go deeper and deeper; I can smell grape skins on my fingers, and I can recall the taste of the fruit (and the fried fish and chips that I ate before the grapes); I can feel the ends of my nails as I tap.

But to judge from the way most classrooms work most of the time, and the way that some work all the time, the inmates – the children anyway – are not invited to think and learn about that outside world – indeed they are discouraged from it. They are persuaded to live, or at least partly live, in the belief that abstract marks on paper – what is called their literacy, their numeracy – have more reality than, let's say, the stones and the muck of the field, or the sand and the pebbles of the shore, or the birds and the clouds, or the sun and the stars of the air, or the somehow still living atmosphere of a ruined church. And, once they have been granted supervised parole, all too often they are persuaded that the worksheet and the notes that they must make score over the medieval walls of a castle.

Children in school think about that world outside the classroom, of course. Watch them any day, in any classroom, the length and breadth of the country. They look out of windows at clouds scudding or sailing, or at traffic moving; at friends in another class running, bowling hoops or kicking balls. Behind their eyes, there are memories of family life and friendship; of holidays and celebrations in winter; of other countries in other continents where they, or their parents, began their lives. All this reminds them of a world that seems now so distant from this box in which they work.

But life goes on in this box as well. Every now and then the door opens, and everyone looks up – some excitement? No, it's only Miss from the office with a message about . . . anything interesting? Only this: Cherie won't be in school till later.

Gone to the dentist. Or it's the headteacher showing someone around. Parents? Boring. Or here's Jeannine from 4F with a message . . . no netball club today. Or perhaps it's the mum who 'hears children read'. That's about Jem and Ellie, they're only on Book 2. So off they go. Sometimes a child has a stroke of luck, and is asked to take a message to another classroom. Children treasure these opportunities for pathetic little getaways. You only have to hold up the register with a questioning look to see raised hands, excited eyes.

So it goes on, with an assumption that all that matters to these children and their educational life exists inside this cuboid. I am going to try to make a case in this book that if more of the time they spend *inside* it was spent thinking about what goes on *outside* it, the work they do *in* it would be stronger; and, second, more importantly, that if they spent more time *outside* it, it would be stronger still, and full, in a literal sense, of life.

The classroom is a semi-permanent, bricks-and-mortar – or concrete-and-glass – statement that children can find out almost all (if not all) that they need to know to prepare them for their working lives in these specially designed boxes. (I use the industrialists' phrasing here, 'their working lives', because there is no pretence in it, as there is now and then among politicians, that schools should be concerned with other parts of the children's lives – or their lives *per se*).

Over the past sixty years, there have been developments in ideas about what knowledge is and how it is transmitted from one generation to another. Sure, there are still 'spelling mornings' when rote learning is demanded. But most educationists, whether implicitly or explicitly, now work as though 'transmission' is a faulty metaphor; that knowledge is not simply handed down (much as that must have seemed 'common sense' to countless generations of teachers); that learning is more complex, and that we have as human beings always interpreted new information in terms of what we already know. For example, we bring to the learning of how to ride a bike all that we have learned, consciously or not, in crawling and walking. And we were not taught to walk. As Denys Thompson wrote in his foreword to Alec Clegg's book *The Excitement of Writing* (1966) 'It is a fallacy that what can be learned can and must be taught.'

We are not taught to crawl, to sit up, to talk . . . is it not likely that writing is something we begin to teach ourselves when we scribble on our first wall? And that that scribbling might be something that teachers should build on? This confidence about classrooms should – though it seldom seems to – provoke a question: Are children not learning before they come to school in the thousands of experiences they have at home? The notion that they aren't should be a strange one for any of us who have both worked in schools and brought children into the world.

Recent developments in education have led to a few small changes in the shapes of classrooms. In the sixties and seventies, for example, English teachers in secondary schools talked about the 'disappearing dais', or read a book with that title (Whitehead 1966, the same year as the Clegg book – a year in the middle of a decade with a reputation, not justified, for setting people free). Or they heard about a book with that title, and they began to move around the room initiating conversations with individual students, rather than preaching as if from a pulpit, or dais. Or it was rumoured that they did. Either way, the classroom survived essentially intact as a preaching box. And like a preaching box, the traditional classroom is essentially a mode of control. It enables the teachers to make sure that the children are as safe as they can make them, but it also ensures that potential learning from outside doesn't interfere with what matters: the prescribed learning inside.

Around the same time that the dais was disappearing, and as if to recognise more flexible and fluent models of learning with younger students, local authorities built open-plan primary schools, where children were, it was said, invited to discover things for themselves. But despite accusations from the political right, which travestied the word 'discover' ('Do children learn to read by a process of osmosis?' became a much-repeated cliché), 'progressive' primary education was rarely put into practice, and soon partitions made of bookshelves, cupboards and display screens brought back the old order: the sealed-off classroom. The idea of team-teaching, when a group of two, three or four teachers might contribute expertise and knowledge to children's discovery of a topic, and how it might encourage understanding of language, of art, of science, of mathematics, of history, of geography, got no purchase on most teachers' practice. There were rumours, malicious and unfounded, I am convinced, that open-plan schools had cost less to build. In any event, 'progressive education' was, in Joni Mitchell's words, 'just a dream some of us had'.

In this book, I see the classroom as the hub of a wheel with spokes leading to other places in the world beyond it, some of which feature in my chapter titles. I want to suggest a central truth: **Teaching children outside a classroom, almost regardless of what we are teaching, increases the vitality of learning.** This is, in part, because of the element of surprise, and I explore this in my chapter on teaching in the school grounds. It is probably easy for teachers to underestimate the joy that a sudden change from school desk to trees and grass can make.

A second reason for freeing children from the classroom is that so much of what both conventional and wider curricula demand of teachers and children is out there. Sociology, local history, geography, architecture? Walk down the streets with your eyes wide open, looking, as Blake says somewhere that we should, 'until it hurts'. History? Mathematics? Look at the shapes in buildings in high streets. Religion? Go to Castle Acre in Norfolk, or to a cathedral or church or mosque or synagogue. Art? Go to the Walker Gallery in Liverpool, or the National in London or the Sainsbury Centre at the University of East Anglia in Norwich, or to the little gallery in or near your local town. Commerce? Visit a Tesco store. I glance over that list, and note with satisfaction that entry to each one of those places named, except for Castle Acre, is free.

Learning outside the classroom does not only mean what I will call 'adventures'. Explorations of HMS Victory, rock climbing, seeing Paris in the spring, skiing in the Austrian mountains – all of these are wonderful things, and children who experience them, and countless other adventures, will be richer emotionally, intellectually, socially and spiritually. But that's not so easy nowadays. Money is tighter than could have been imagined a decade ago; teachers have much more on their minds than they used to, and they are working longer hours; successive governments emphasise 'core subjects' to the necessary relegation of everything else. And an increased and, some would say, neurotic emphasis on children's security and the resulting paperwork has driven many teachers to write such projects off. One teacher told me that staff at the Royal Shakespeare Company in Stratford issue a large booklet of guidance to help teachers fill in risk assessment forms. One section mentions 'Swan attack – danger slight'.

I remember weeks camping with children in Hampshire, and visiting HMS Victory, Silverton Open-Air Museum and the Roman mosaics at Fishbourne; other weeks walking over Brunel's Great Eastern, or exploring Winchester Cathedral; and I remember these as some of the most fulfilling times of my professional life. It is unjust that children today should be deprived of such riches as these, riches that their parents and grandparents enjoyed and even, in many cases, took for granted.

However, there is an environment that is part of the world beyond the classroom on every school's doorstep, whether it is a village, a town or a city, and I'll come to it shortly. But, after a brief chapter about writing, I begin in a literally homely way.

1

Writing and thinking

1 Writing and making it better

This book is concerned, above all, with words. This is because of my certainty that writing is the most powerful medium for learning about almost anything. It enables children to explore not just the words that they consider, reject or use; not just the subject they are writing about; but, critically, they are learning about the relationship they have with both their language and the subject of their writing.

Writing is not, pre-eminently, a *record* of learning. It is a part, and a vital part, of the *process* of learning. Thus, it doesn't merely record our thoughts, our discoveries, our meditations, though it does do that sometimes. It modifies them; it enriches them; it makes them clearer and yet, paradoxical as it might seem, it adds to them and makes them more complex. However confusing those thoughts, discoveries and meditations are, writing words down makes them graspable. While before we wrote there was an intangible cloudlike presence in our head, writing has given that presence a shape on which we can meditate further. We look at the paper, and discover that our thinking has at last some kind of local habitation, some kind of name.

I will emphasise in several places in this book the importance of the different stages of writing: getting some words down fast, before they are forgotten; then jotting in the margins and in the gaps between these initial notes; redrafting. Our first words written down – even on a shopping list – are almost always provisional. Those words are never, or are rarely, quite what we meant to say. They are, as football managers say of inexperienced players 'not the finished article'. Much of what we learn as we write is done at the stage when we examine what we have written with a pencil in hand, ready to add and score out; all this with questions in mind. And when we do this, we find that we write better: we find more appropriate words, words that convey a thought as lucidly as possible. The second draft comes into being, not in copying out with spelling and punctuation corrections, but in the margins of the first draft; or in the spaces between the lines; or in rings at the bottom of the page, with arrows showing where new words, or sentences, or parts of sentences, are to go. Then we can make a second copy of our work.

To help this second-drafting we might, as teachers, usefully encourage the children to ask some open-ended questions:

Is what I have written true? Have I said what I meant to say?

Teachers need to teach children that, just as in life we should all tell the truth, so they (and we) should tell it in our writing. This teaching can be given extra force by the fact that a lie written down sometimes hangs around for a long time and does even greater damage than a spoken lie. (The obvious problem with this – that all of us tell lies in life, whether with good or bad intentions – need not detain us here.) The poet Wendy Cope once said on Radio 4 (quoted in the book *As the Poet Said*, edited by Tony Curtis) 'When a poem doesn't work, the first question to ask yourself is "Am I telling the truth?"'

One of the most common untruths that children fall for is caused by the forced rhyme, as in this example from a 'poem' a child wrote on 'Water' for a national competition: 'It comes to us as rain hail or snow / And when it is finished then it does go'. When children ask me in the normal course of things 'Can I make it rhyme?' there are two possible responses. The first is: 'If you tell the truth with your rhyme, yes.' This is only any use when the class is experienced in writing well; when their thinking about writing is sufficiently sophisticated. The second response is 'No.' The poet Seamus Heaney once demurred on hearing praise for one of his earliest poems. He had, he said, been seduced by the rhyme. The story is told in *Stepping Stones: Interviews with Seamus Heaney* by Dennis O'Driscoll. Heaney had overcooked an emotion by ending a stanza with 'hate' because earlier lines had ended with 'wait' and 'late'.

It isn't really fair, perhaps, banning rhyme for children. After all, they are surrounded by it in advertising; in songs; in nursery, playground and counting-out rhymes; and, indeed, in most of the poems teachers introduce them to. But it is difficult to teach them the difference between the plonking irrelevance of the rhyme quoted above and the natural rightness of, say, this one anonymous example:

> How many miles to Babylon?
> Three score and ten.
> Shall we get there by candlelight?
> Yes, and back again.
> We shall get there by candlelight
> If your heels are nimble and light.

With its alternative ending:

> Open your gates as wide as the sky
> And let the king and his men pass by.

Or in Scotland:

> Here's a beck and here's a boo,
> Open your gates and let us through.

(For hundreds of other such traditional verses, see *The Singing Game*, by Opie and Opie.)

I explain two other techniques, alliteration and assonance. The children usually know about the former but not the latter. These techniques are relatively easy to understand and they are less open to abuse, we might say. Like rhyme, they make a kind of music, and once children accept that putting 'goat' at the end of a line because the previous line ends with 'throat' or 'float' or 'moat' or 'boat' or 'note' is not such a good idea, they make good use of repeated consonantal or vowel sounds. A famous line of Tennyson's – 'murmuring of innumerable bees', from 'The Princess' – illustrates these two techniques; there is a more subtle example from Wordsworth's 'I wandered lonely as a cloud' in Chapter 3 (see p 21).

Have I written any clichés?

I don't know why it has never been part of the national curriculum to teach children first to recognise clichés and then to delete them. In children's writing, 'birds twitter prettily', lions 'leap upon their prey' and babies are 'cute', much as football managers 'take each day as it comes' and duplicitous politicians 'make things abundantly clear' even as they blow smoke over the truth. I mock these and other clichés, and then deliver a brief lecture on news 'spreading like wildfire' and the like. Sometimes we have cliché-hunting sessions with newspapers. It surprises me sometimes to see clichés on classroom walls presented as examples of good practice: 'Here is one way to begin a story: "Once upon a time in a country a long way away there lived a beautiful princess . . .".'

Could I put this better?

I call this activity 'Editing Friends'. I ask children to read their writing to each other in pairs. They should do this at least twice, with one child at first listening, and then, on the second and further readings, asking questions that will help her partner to improve the work. Often this helps them sharpen the focus. Someone has written 'trees', for example, or 'birds', or 'flowers', and their editing friend asks, 'What kind of trees (or birds, or flowers) were they? . . . What colour were the roses?' When one child has written the lion/prey cliché, the other should insist on her naming the prey – just by thinking about it, or by going to a reference book about animals. Or by using the Internet. Then I get children to think of details that will add colour to their writing; to check to see if they have used the same word more than once; or to see if there isn't a better word than the one they've used. Children should get used to doing this for each other as editing friends.

Are there any unnecessary words in my writing?

Many classrooms have notices on the wall with 'a list of interesting adjectives'. But in fact fluent writers in primary schools often use too many adjectives, often pairing one with another that has a similar, if not identical, meaning, or else pairing two adjectives where one covers the meaning of the other, as in the famous example 'It was a dark and stormy night': all stormy nights are dark, except during the lightning flashes. These children need not to be alert for more adjectives but to make sure that their nouns and verbs – the bones and muscles of writing respectively – should be well chosen. Many adjectives (and adverbs) are surplus fat. Other unnecessary words are nouns repeated when a pronoun would do the job better: this is easily dealt with if children are taught to read their writing back to themselves for the sound of it. 'My Dad', for example, is often repeated when 'he' would work.

2 Really thinking

The words 'think' and 'thought' will come up many times in this book. But all too often, when teachers ask children to think, they really mean 'guess', as in (looking at stained glass in a church, for example) 'What do you think those windows are for?' or 'How are those windows different from the ones at school?' Hands shoot up. Can a child with his hand in the air think? I believe it is unlikely: his or her mind is entirely focussed on getting attention. A class of children faced with (a) a question and (b) the expectation that one of them will come up with an immediate and correct answer is competing, not learning, not thinking. The children are not reflecting on objects – those stained glass windows, say – and relating what they are learning about them to what they know already. And that is what I mean by thinking: it is the bringing of old knowledge into the presence of new phenomena, and interpreting the new in the light of the old.

I try to introduce into the classroom a kind of purposeful silence. This has nothing to do with the kind of silence we impose on a class while we call the register, or take part in a fire drill, or quite simply when we find that the level of noise is hurting our ears. It is a time when there will be no sound except that of pens moving on paper or (rather obscurely, I admit) the sound of brains working. The sound of feelings about something being explored. I often say to children: when I clap my hands, I am going to change this classroom from being a classroom into being a study – a study where twenty-odd writers (I always add one, for me – I am going to try to write too) are working. In silence. No talking. No music. Nothing. And the minds think. And the pens and pencils move. This doesn't have to last long – ten minutes say – to have a beneficial effect on writing. One poem written in the grip of this silence went like this:

> Silence is when you can hear things.
> Listen!
> You can hear a rose growing.
> Listen!
> You can hear a cat breathing.
> Listen!
> You can hear an ant stop, looking to see where it is.
> Listen!
> You can hear yourself blink!

2

At home

Eloise's news January 28th

Our babby brother jams Michel
was born on crismas day
and I rote about it in my news

but all my teacher did
was put in capitals and full stops
and corect my spelling

(FS)

'Nil on entry.' I saw this written at the foot of a report on a five-year-old. She had started the week before in the reception class in the primary school where I was the headteacher. It reminded me then, as it does now, of that bleak instruction most of us have seen clipped onto the ends of hospital beds: 'Nil by mouth.' The latter instruction is imperative and necessary in its context, but the nihilism of the former is hard (even to this day) for me to forgive.

Or, as you can tell, to forget. This was over twenty years ago. And things have, of course (or so I have heard and do in part believe) improved. But even so, I have often heard the same judgment made about children since, if in more subtle terms. When coffee time arrives on the first day of term, teachers and learning support assistants (LSAs) congregate, apparently caffeine-parched, in the staffroom. Then somebody is sure to tell the Special Needs Co-ordinator, 'You've got plenty to work with in my new class.' Somebody else says, 'I've got someone special for you . . .'.

Someone? And that child's name – Cheryl, say – is exchanged, and her reputation, tainted on her first morning in school, will go before her. From now on she is defined not by her intellectual ability (though that would be bad enough) but (and this is far worse) by how that ability was assessed before morning break on the first day of her first term. Innocent as she is of the fact, she is in a similar position to a football team running onto the pitch already 0–2 down.

These comments were made about children diagnosed as having 'special educational needs'. In past decades, the term would have been 'retarded' or 'backward'. Charles Dickens' favourite character, David Copperfield, had to walk round his school with a placard round his neck: HE BITES. These children have been labelled too, and the results will become clear soon enough: they will be drawn out of normal lessons to work on 'phonics' and 'reading skills' in corridors with parents, and treated differently from the other children in subtle ways – not meeting the visiting story-teller, for example. Certain experiences will be deemed beyond them.

These children undoubtedly feel the rougher end of this stereotyping. But all children diagnosed early in their school lives are dealt a raw deal. Another child is deemed in the same eye blink of time as being ready for the first book of a reading scheme. This child too bears the weight of a label. She is 'bright', 'able', 'gifted and talented' ('g & t' in that ludicrous abbreviation), and has much to live up to after less than two hours in school.

Neither of these assessments is fair. Neither of them even pretends to take into account any child's learning before she enters the classroom. The 'able reader' may well have read, with different but always increasing levels of competence, a hundred books before arriving at school, but Book 2 in the reading scheme will be her diet in her first week at school. The niece of a friend of mine had the blessing of artists for parents, and under their guidance she had been drawing since she could hold a pencil. Each tree she drew had in winter the bare angular anatomy of branches; and had every May a 'full-grown thickness' (Larkin's phrase from 'The Trees', in his *Collected Poems*). She came home during her first week at school to her mother and father with a lollipop tree drawing and explained: 'That's how you draw trees at school.'

This is one way that schools can be anti-educational in their underrating and implicit dismissal of all learning experienced outside them. I see this when headteachers complain about children being taken out of school during term time. When my eight-year-old son was walking round Malta exploring fragments of prehistory, churches, art galleries and beaches during an Autumn term – I was on a term's break from a headship a few years ago (most of the term was taken up with a course) – he was learning in an immeasurable, random but more powerful way more than he would have been learning in the relatively sterile atmosphere of the classroom. I have watched families on holiday in the Sea Life Centre at Hunstanton in the days before the summer holidays began (cheaper then, of course), and I would gladly have challenged those headteachers: what would you provide at the end of July that is more engaging, more educational than this?

Children learn with their parents at home, on visits to the park, on family visits, on holidays . . . . With some observations and some reflection, any parent can see how much of a slander on the child and family life that the teacher-talk I've quoted at the beginning of this chapter is. Malachi (I am thinking of a particular baby) recognised the voices of his parents within a few hours. In a few days, he was turning his head at the sound of the known voices of aunts, uncles and grandparents arriving at the front door. Soon he learned how to express enjoyment or disgust at new food; he once, at the age of about four months, told his mother with frowns and growls (I was watching and listening) something like: No, Mummy, thank you, I do *not* want to be read that story, I want another one, yes, *that* one. All this learning is part of my motivation for Chapter 2 of this book: learning at home is the most significant part of the learning beyond the school fence. It isn't measurable, of course, and that is one reason why it is downplayed.

And anyone who believes that much pre-school experience is poverty-stricken, especially in terms of language, should read Gordon Wells' book *The Meaning Makers* (1986), especially his pages on five-year-old Rosie (pp 94–101), who talks freely at home but who is tongue-tied at school, because school has started the unrelenting process of giving her the language equivalent of the lollipop tree, and legitimising only certain kinds of talk: talk with strange adults, talk about new subjects, literacy and numeracy. We might usefully wonder: how does a Special Educational Needs Co-ordinator (SENCO) appear to a five-year-old in her first term? What sense does the SENCO's language make? Almost all children have experienced language before they come to school that is richer and wider than anything any reading scheme can offer. Another book that demonstrates this is *Young Children Learning* by Barbara Tizard and Martin Hughes. These researchers heard rich conversations between mothers and four-year-olds at home – richer than any they heard at school.

Getting writing out of the home experience

I am not concerned here with teaching literally outside the classroom. That comes in the rest of this book. In this chapter, my subject is ensuring that children have opportunities to remember all family experiences, whether in the house or outside it, and to reflect on them and to write about them. With this work, even though their bodies are in the classroom, their minds and hearts are outside it. Here, for example, is a seven-year-old discovering through writing yet more of the abundant and incomprehensible joy a family event had given her a few days ago. She recollects (re-collects) her emotions in tranquillity:

> our babby jams Michel was born on crismas day

and on the paper her teacher had corrected spelling and put in conventional punctuation. There was no evidence that the teacher had given a moment's thought to how this child had experienced not only a surprise, and not any old surprise, but one that was a milestone in her life, and a surprise on Christmas Day, a day when, she had heard, another baby had been born; or that she had considered that the writer was so keen to get her news down onto paper that she'd had no time to worry about commas and full stops – that the news was more important, for once at least, than such details. I photocopied the writing (I carried it around for a while until it disintegrated along the fold lines) and brought it home and wrote the angry little poem I've included at the beginning of this chapter. I reflected then and I reflect now: almost everything that happens to children in the lives they live outside school is ignored in the classroom. Here the teacher had asked the children to write about a hackneyed subject – 'What happened in the holidays?' – and she had got in return far more than she deserved; and her response fell far below what it ought to have been.

This chapter is really no more than a plea to give greater attention to what happens in children's family lives. We should do this, first, out of good manners; second, because a child may need an adult outside the family to share in a celebration or in a sadness; and third, because experiences at home are fruit to be picked by us in helping children to improve their communication, especially in speech and writing.

Another child wrote in one of my sessions:

I remember the time when my daddy could not come to the fathers' afternoon because it was my great-grandmother's funeral . . .

I said, 'Your great grandmother? She must've been very old.' 'Yes,' said the girl. 'And my great-grandfather is still alive and he is 94!' Then she added that new sentence to her writing. This little moment of celebration only came about because I had managed – not always easy in the modern classroom – to read her writing with due attention.

This girl was one of a group of 'talented writers' – I prefer the term 'keen writers', but find it difficult to make it stick – aged between eight and ten years. They attended Springfield Junior School in Ipswich, and because I worked with them over a long period, they appear many times in this book. I had asked them for unusual things that had happened 'away from school'. Here are some more examples of their writing.

I remember when I was in South Africa and I saw a massive lizard that shot through the bushes and I jumped back in fear.

I remember when I went to a forest near a lake and I saw a water vole in a glass bottle being eaten by black and yellow bugs.

I remember walking in the tunnels of the Tampa Bay Stadium and I saw a rat in a popcorn machine.

And another boy remembered a holiday and wrote notes about a car journey that ended up like this:

Catseyes

You gleam
in the middle of the road
staring blankly into nothingness
guiding but not moving
as I drive along.
I see your steady beat
going light, dark, light, dark
eating up the darkness
and spitting out light.

There is a theme in this book which I will suggest by example rather than in a more specific way. If we want the best writing from our children, wherever we and wherever they are, we have to be open about some of our own experiences. I am going to use an example of my own writing to make this point. Sometime after my mother died and I had lost both my parents it became an urgent matter to record memories of the place where she'd been born. I had no ideas of trying to publish what I would produce: it was for my benefit only. It was part of the process of understanding that my mother's absence was now her manner of appearing to me. I had visited the farmstead in Ballyjamesduff in County Cavan in Ireland, both as a child and as an adolescent. It had always been part of her to me, but now it became much more seriously so because I knew that it was unlikely I would ever see it again.

And there would be no chance now of finding out things, of getting information from my mother – things that seemed unimportant when she was alive, but which now mattered to me. I would have to interpret the scanty data I had about the place *for myself*. And, worse, *by* myself. The layout of the farmhouse, the fields and the outlying buildings. The cigarettes (Players untipped, I now remember) that my grandfather smoked. The livestock that he and one of my uncles – the sibling, one of eight, who hadn't left – kept. Even the names of my mother's seven brothers and sisters in the right order . . .

Recalling visits as a child in the nineteen-fifties and as a teenager in the sixties, I wrote this:

The staircase is a tall room of its own, entirely wooden. It has no floor, or rather it has ten little ones, spiralling upwards, the steps that take you up to where you sleep. It is dark because (and this always interests me) there are doors both at the bottom and the top.

There's a parlour at the front of the house downstairs where you never go, except on Sunday evenings. Then my mother plays hymns on the piano, her eyes screwed intently on the music. As she will tell me, years later, she doesn't play the piano very well. Indeed, I never saw her play it anywhere else.

This piano is also a pianola. You feed into the back of it what looks like Braille on rolls roughly the size and shape of large corn-on-the-cobs, and magically the piano plays, the keys jumping up and down. You can sit at the piano and pretend to be playing. This was fun then, and to think of it is funny now. The piano must have been, for my mother's family, as close as possible to a record player, to a stereo, to a video, to a DVD. They made, as they say, their own entertainment then.

The room smelt of polish, so someone must have gone in there during the week.

On weekdays after work, my granddad and my uncle Stanley pull their boots off outside a kitchen door. I don't remember them doing this. I suppose I imagine it. Nor do I remember an incident that my mother told me about. Once, when I was very small, I carried a piglet into the kitchen to show my grandma. She hit me, and my mother reproached her. I don't remember this, of course, but that is what my mother told me. How many memories that people have are merely what they have been told? Or even recollected from photographs, those truthful lies?

The farmy smell of cows is a mixture, I suppose now, of milk and dung. There's a photograph, probably taken by my father, who loved his twin lens reflex camera, of my cousin Joan. She runs to the byre with an empty bucket. She will have crouched beside the cow, jetting the milk from the teats onto the zinc with a wet clang. I had a go once. Years later I took my son to a milking machine that worked on twenty-odd cows at once. In Ireland, I was alone with my cousin and one cow with her swollen udders and her slithery teats.

And, disgusting to us London children, the toilet is outside.

In the barn there's a long blade leaning on the wall, dangerous with its silver teeth, where my brother cuts himself, and has to be taken to hospital. I can see his thigh now, weeping little scarlet tears: blood. Or can I? Am I recalling what I have been told?

I knew that every child in the group would arrive at a solemn time when he or she, as I had, would feel the need to recall details about late parents, late grandparents, late great-grandparents, and here was a way of giving them a chance to practise a mode of writing that might help them. But it was a mode of writing, with its necessary darkness, with its risks, that was rarely going to be taught in schools. I decided to have a go: this was, of course, writing in the classroom, but all the force behind it came from somewhere I would never know – the children's homes.

It would have been crude and dangerous to ask the children to remember a person. I wanted them to begin at a slight distance, to approach someone at an angle. A room might serve as an object that stood for someone. That's how I began. I asked my group of keen writers to recall a room they remembered. They were to consider its decor, its furnishings, experiences they remember taking place in the room and, above all, a person they associated with that room. We called the pieces that they produced 'The Room from the Past'. I told them some details of the story I've given above.

> When I stepped into this room I thought the carpet was sweet-smelling. The smell of flowers came from the windows.
>
> The sound of the family singing songs to the karaoke and where I keep saying Mum, Mum. They sang the silliest songs and I giggled loud and clear. My granddad sang too. That made me embarrassed. They've got it on tape and it's so funny.
>
> I remember the little baby toy I waddle in and play arguments with my cousin. The little toys, I had been chucking them from here and there. The chairs I sank into, the sofa a lot. I climbed on to little coffee tables and they shouted Get off, you'll break it. The tv was old but I didn't care. The best thing was, I nap, I sleep for as long as I would like. I loved the living room when I was young. It was very cool.

I once watched a baby crawling some months after he had become proficient at walking. A friend said 'He's remembering the good times.' My friend was right: even a baby has a nostalgia for earlier stages in life when the only option was to crawl. In this piece, the writer is remembering the good times, and there will have been a warmth inside her as she wrote these words. If we look closer than we usually do at children's writing, we might note the sentence that begins 'They've got it on tape . . .' has been unwittingly anticipated in the present tense verb 'keep': the family play this tape from time to time. And we can almost hear her mother telling her how the little girl loved her nap when she could sleep for as long as she wanted.

There has been page after page published about personal, social and moral education during the last thirty years, some by me. I once saw an 'audit' of PSE skills. But here is the centre of it, the place where it starts: a child's awareness of her place in her family, and an extended opportunity to reflect on it, to write about it, to discuss it with a teacher and other children. And to celebrate it. And this writing with the warmth and memories enshrined in it will help this writer when there are darker days.

I had emphasised working with paragraphs in the introduction to this lesson. I had also called the children's attention to the way using the senses enriches their work. This next writer managed her memories in a more controlled way; she employed her senses well, even the tactile sense ('the fast friction of my hands' is a terrific phrase):

When I first went upstairs to the decking I saw a big cabin-like house, number 68, all on one level. I pulled open the big glass sliding door and I saw two large sofas with a big fireplace with a big cage surrounding it. I loved it.

I could smell wood and the smell of the fire and the smoke rising. I could smell the pine trees from the woods outside and a bonfire far away.

I could feel the velvety chair and when I knelt down at the fire and rubbed my hands together I could feel the warmth of the fire and the fast friction of my hands.

I could hear the wind passing through the trees out of my bedroom window making a loud rustling sound.

We used to play board games on the carpet and my little brother used to get on my back when I was on all fours and I would crawl along.

The place belonged to my great auntie and she let us stay there for a few days.

That is another example of a writer remembering the good times, encapsulated in that image of a child crawling along with her little brother on her back. When I saw her again, I pointed out that the lines 'I could smell wood and the smell of the fire and the smoke rising. I could smell the pine trees from the woods outside and a bonfire far away' did their work even more effectively if she didn't use the word 'smell' more than once. She recast them like this: 'I could smell wood. And the fire and the smoke rose nearby. And there were pine trees as well, and a bonfire far away.' It is best that young writers write about the senses without using the obvious words. A sentence like 'In the distance I could hear lorries rumbling past' (which comes up soon) is much better recast as 'Lorries rumbled past in the distance.'

Thinking about a room has enabled the next writer to reflect on her great grandma:

The light brown walls just stand proud and tall. At the front of the room was the dark brown bookcase filled up with books from top to bottom, which had an occasional picture of me on it.

The sofas were comfy but not too comfy, with pin pricks of white in the misty brown.

The telly was old and box-shaped as well as being grey. It was right on top of a short and stumpy sideboard in which were old dusty video tapes and a big dusty hanging cream light.

That was my great grandma's front room.

A boy wrote:

When I first entered the room, I was surprised how small it was. It was a tiny bedroom with a TV hanging on the wall and a few models on the window sill.

The smells were glorious. It smelt like Tommy (a greyhound), a little bit of wine and of biscuits. I smelt a hint of dirty socks, also beer.

I saw the window open so I went to stand by it with a warm welcome from a blackbird song. In the distance I could hear lorries rumbling past. I could also hear Tommy running around the garden.

There were no decorations. Just a plain wall with a few sploshes of paint on. The only furniture were dragon models, a TV and a bedside cabinet. It's the smallest bedroom I've ever seen!

It's my Nan's bedroom and I love it.

In another session I explained to the writers that, in writing about those rooms, they were writing autobiography, which was a 'special case' of biography – or, as it is often called today, 'life writing'. Keeping a journal is an easy task to give oneself, but a notoriously difficult one to keep up. The empty pages stretch forbiddingly into the distance, promising more than anything a sense of mild guilt at our failure to write on them. I decided we would see this exercise as notes: things to be written down when they came to mind. For one starter, I read children a piece from the *Confessions* of Augustine of Hippo. He was a Christian church father who lived from 354–430. This book is said to be the first example in literature of a writer examining his own soul. Be that as it may, Augustine is obsessed with his own sins – even the sins of his childhood. I have adapted this passage from the translation given in Michael Rosen's *Penguin Book of Childhood*:

There was a pear tree near the vineyard on our farm. It was loaded with fruit, unpleasant to look at and unpleasant to taste as well. Late one night the gang of boys I used to hang around with ran off and shook and shook at the tree till many of the pears fell to the ground. We had stayed out late, long after the time when our parents would have been expecting us home. That was our usual evil habit.

We carried the pears away. We didn't eat them – we threw them at the pigs. We may have eaten a few, but the pleasure we got from this escapade was in doing something that we were not allowed to do, something that was forbidden.

Augustine notes how he and the boys took no pleasure in the act except insofar as it was forbidden. I pointed this out to the children – 'Do you do some things *just because they're naughty?*' Invariably some of them slowly nod their heads. We then talked in groups about 'naughty things' that we remembered doing. I stressed that word – 'naughty' – now exclusively applied to children's deeds, because I didn't want to hear about serious anti-social behaviour – thieving, bullying and so on (not that anything of that nature was likely with this group). I fully accept that school should be a place where such deeds and their consequences are discussed, but my lesson was not tooled up for it, and I did not know the children well enough.

It all started when my dad dug a hole at the bottom of the garden, put a black sheet over it, and filled it with water to make a pond. He was very pleased when he found a toad in it.

Sometime later my auntie, uncle and two cousins came round to play. After a while we (that is, me, Rachel my sister and my cousins, Milly and Michaela) went down to the bottom of the garden to the pond. We started by giving worms rides on the old plastic container and pushing them across the pond to each other. But then we turned our attention to getting some big sticks to dig with. Then we thought of pushing the dirt from underneath the big stones to weigh the black sheet down, to watch it go all cloudy, as if we were builders or something.

We were having great fun with our imaginary building and excavating when Uncle James came down to see what we were up to. He called to Dad to come and take a look. 'Mark, I think you should come over, it's not that clear pond you showed me earlier.' Auntie Tracy said to him, 'Don't tell tales, Jamie.'

'Yeah, don't tell tales' we retorted. But too late. Dad had come down to look at the pond. He was very annoyed. 'It'd better have settled by the time we get back from the playground!' he cried.

I was a bit slower than the others so I heard what mum and dad were saying. 'I'm not very impressed. They'll be in more trouble if they stir it up again!'

Luckily the pond had pretty much cleared, and the mud had settled when we came back, but it was a close call.

I like to show children that they can have a dramatic effect on what they have written simply by changing the tense from the past (the default tense used to record memories unless an alternative is offered) to the present. I often play with this with my own writing: indeed, I wrote the passage above about the Irish farmhouse in the past tense originally. This change usually has a cinematic effect: you seem to be seeing something happen in close-up through the lens of a hand-held camera, as in this version of the last piece:

It all starts when my dad digs a hole at the bottom of the garden, puts a black sheet over it, and fills it with water to make a pond. He is very pleased when he finds a toad in it.

Sometime later my auntie, uncle and two cousins come round to play. After a while we (that is, me, Ruby my sister and my cousins, Maddy and Daisy) go down to the bottom of the garden to the pond. We start by giving worms rides on the old plastic container and pushing them across the pond to each other. But then we turn our attention to getting some big sticks to dig with. Then we think of pushing the dirt from underneath the big stones to weigh the black sheet down, to watch it go all cloudy, as if we are builders or something.

We are having great fun with our imaginary building and excavating when Uncle James comes down to see what we are up to. He calls to Dad to come and take a look. 'Mark, I think you should come over, it's not that clear pond you showed me earlier.' Auntie Tracy says to him, 'Don't tell tales, Jamie.'

'Yeah, don't tell tales' we retort. But too late. Dad has come down to look at the pond. He is very annoyed. 'It'd better have settled by the time we get back from the playground!' he cries.

I am a bit slower than the others so I hear what mum and dad are saying. 'I'm not very impressed. They'll be in more trouble if they stir it up again!'

Luckily the pond has pretty much cleared, and the mud has settled when we come back, but it's a close call!

That piece serves as a vivid description of children at play. Another confession read like this:

When I was about 3 or 4 I watched Tracey Beaker and somebody make a contraption which trapped someone who hit it.

So I thought of making my own contraption that dropped a toy dagger on someone's head when they hit a piece of long thin string. I went to my bedroom and planned the whole thing, of how it worked.

I waited till someone came upstairs and went into their room. Then I barricaded their (my sister's) room so I could make it. It took about half an hour to make but I finished and unbarricaded her room and she ran downstairs to tell mum about the barricading and she hit the trap. The toy dagger hit her right on the head.

I got told off real bad and they destroyed my contraption but I knew they were proud of how ingenious I was.

Later, these writers wrote about an event that, as I put it to them, made a big difference in their lives; made them feel that things would never be the same again. I told them about the births of my son and then *his* son, my grandson; about the deaths of my parents; and how those events made my life take new directions. I was prepared for writing that showed evidence of children looking deep into themselves, and I knew that they might not find this altogether comfortable.

This writer (she told the story on p 16 about her father's pond) tended to behave as a private person in the regular writing sessions, making few verbal contributions, but writing with energy and fluency, nearly always producing work at a slight angle to the conventional, and with occasional hints of maturity; even a kind of wryness unusual in children ('He is very pleased when he finds a toad in it'). She took a special interest in the poems I read to begin each session, and in any talk about the business of writing. Now she wrote:

It all started on December 23rd 2008, the day before Christmas Eve. We were all very excited about tomorrow and the day after. Dad came home and said 'Eleanor, Rachel, we've got something to tell you.'

I started to think of things that might have happened.

'Has Alfred died? Are you getting divorced?' etc etc.

'No' said Dad simply. 'What happens when people get old?' he asked.

'They die' I said.

'Yes' Dad said. 'Someone has died.'

'Grandma Geraldine?' I asked.

'No' answered Dad.

'Who?' I persisted.

'Grandad Grahame' said Dad quietly.

The moment Dad told us everything changed. Rachel burst into tears, so did Mum. I don't know if this makes me a bad person or anything, but I didn't, even though I was very sad.

Grandad invited us for sleepovers, took us up to the playground, spoiled us rotten when it came to sweets and chocolate and cakes etc., but now we couldn't see him anymore, and no, it wasn't just the sweets and chocolate and cakes that made me sad. I just felt sad because I couldn't see him anymore.

We always have a family get together round my cousin's house on 23rd December now, and we always have a toast to Grandad Grahame.

Another autobiographical note comes from the same session:

It was the day after Valentines Day 2010 when it all started. In the morning at 8 o'clock mum and dad called me and Sammy, my big brother, downstairs so they could talk to us.

Suddenly I began to feel tense because of the way they were talking. It was like they couldn't get it out of their mouths.

Finally, when mum and dad said it, me and Sammy had a huge shock and it was that my mum and dad said they were going to be divorced from that day on.

Now my dad has a girlfriend. Her name is Jenny. My dad and her are very closely in love.

I'm used to it now but still very sad and things are very different.

Sometimes I think my mum's got a boyfriend but she says she hasn't so she hasn't.

These children have heard news from the edge. Grandad is dead. Mum and Dad are splitting up. In my experience as a teacher, I have found only one activity that brings any kind of partial resolution to the experiences described in these pieces, some way of getting them into some kind of order, however temporary. Art, Dance and Drama have a role, and my own tradition and its beliefs tell me that with its unique and dubious certainty Religious Education should have one too, if only in prayer. But Jairus's daughter in St Mark's Gospel 5:21–43 came back from the dead, and Grandad Grahame didn't. Detailed, inspirational work in writing in the primary school is essential if children are to grow up with some protection against the slings and arrows.

'I don't know if this makes me a bad person or anything, but I didn't'. How honest children are. The sentimental adult weeps when the situation conventionally demands it, but the honest child doesn't, and then writes down that she didn't, and then, looking around her, and remembering looking around her, she wonders why she didn't. If she goes on like this, pushing her honesty through the adolescent years when conventional responses will be expected of her, she will continue to be a writer, and she will develop some armour against the viciousness of sentimentality.

One boy brought into school words spoken by his mother in answer to the question: 'What is having babies like?' Under my guidance (no more than the stanza titles), he made them into this concise little document:

Having babies

Before

worried
afraid
excited

happy
anxious

After

overjoyed
tired
scared
apprehensive

Another child wrote this:

> It all started on 7.11.02 when my mum went into hospital to have me but they sent her back. Then on the 8.11.02 my mum gave birth to me, Ellie Louise Barker. Due to the fact that my mum and dad had different blood types I was born yellow. For about a week I was put under a special lamp with a red sun shade all over my head. I only wore a nappy. I only wore a nappy in that space of time.

This is a child celebrating her survival: what bigger subject could there be for her writing? In it, we can hear the rhythms of her parents' speech, especially in her proud recording of her full name. She provides her teacher here with an opportunity, not to correct her punctuation, but to share in that celebration; just as Eloise did at the beginning of this chapter. But Eloise, unlike Ellie, was let down. As Eloise in my poem in Chapter 10 (p 100) was in the castle by Mr Barret, who only cared about worksheets.

3

On the playground

I gazed – and gazed – but little thought
What wealth the show to me had brought.
             (Wordsworth, 'I wandered lonely as a cloud')

Happy are those who see beauty in modest spots where others see nothing.
             (Camille Pissarro)

Clouds

      I'd like to be
      John Constable
and make studies of them. The way
they're like language, changing, but not
suddenly; and something for all
      humankind to own.

      I love the words:
      cumulus, heaped,
piled; cirrus, tufted filament;
stratus, laid down like a field
of snow; nimbus, a pagan
      godling's splendour.

      Look up and look
      until it hurts
at the million-patterned flag that
was grey yesterday, that today's
a bright silver tinged with the gold
      of a hidden sun.
             (FS)

It has been a dreary winter. I'm driving home from work one Friday – it's early
evening, and I've come a long way, about ninety miles. As I wait in a traffic jam in
drizzly weather on one of those artery roads that any town requires to get people in

and out of it, I glance out of my window. Catkins hang by the roadside under lamp-light and glisten in the rain. A vague memory of my primary schooldays . . . yes, a nature walk with Miss? . . . where? . . . Jeanette Miles holding my hand, like we did for country dancing (I wonder what happened to her . . .)? Anyhow, catkins hang there, and they are, decades after my primary school years when Miss pointed them out to me, the first intimations of spring and my heart suddenly lifts.

The next day is one of my church-crawling days, and I come upon snowdrops in the gloomy northern side of a country churchyard, All Saints Waldringfield in Suffolk. Signs of hope. Whiteness that is like snow, but isn't: a symbol of hope for generations of inhabitants of this island. In Philip Larkin's phrases from the poem 'First Sight', 'Earth's immeasurable surprise' is growing 'utterly unlike the snow'.

And then, comes March, and . . .

> host[s] of golden daffodils
> Beside the lake, beneath the trees,
> Fluttering and dancing in the breeze.

Wordsworth's poem seems hackneyed to many. The line 'I wandered lonely as a cloud', along with 'Hey nonny no', is a hand-me-down example – or cliché – of what irritates so many adults: poetry is precious ('very affected in speech, manners or behaviour' – *Collins Dictionary*). It's unworldly, it's somehow – in a bad way – a skirt thing, or – also in a bad way – a church thing. Poetry is something a bookish kind of chap does when he should be kicking or throwing or bowling or catching a ball. And now, in the twenty-first century, too much of this poem's lexicon is dated. And other parts are altered in meaning by modern usage: 'twinkle', 'glee', 'gay', 'jocund' – all of these are for different reasons problematic. It's a high count in a poem of only some two hundred words. Could you read it (I ask myself) to fifteen-year-olds?

But it is, nevertheless, fresh to young children. I was surprised as I read it to find one group's attention total. I read it a second time with half an eye on my audience and felt that their excitement was palpable at the comparison with the Milky Way, at the words 'Ten thousand' and at the lovely ending with its so-satisfying clip of the final rhyme – 'And then my heart with pleasure fills, / And dances with the daffodils' – where these two lines present the core of the poet's Romantic belief that he and Nature are one.

The children had set me an example, and later, at home, I tried to read the poem as if I had never come across it before. And, in spite of the archaisms, the pathetic fallacy (is a cloud really lonely? Are the daffs really gleeful?) it is indeed a marvellous poem. That repetition of 'gazed' is just right; and something that I could usefully point out to the children struck me – the subtlety of Wordsworth's alliteration: '**h**igh . . . **h**ills', 'gol**d**en **D**affodils', which compares favourably with the Tennyson example I gave in Chapter 1 (p 7).

Of course it helped that behind me and in full view of the children there was indeed a host of daffodils – not ten thousand, but maybe ten hundred, sharing a patch of earth beside a school playground with some purple and some yellow crocuses. From now onwards, I will take in any fat anthology of English verse (Christopher Ricks' *Oxford Book*, for example) and read this poem to the children, and hope to find myself in a setting where they can listen to the words and gaze as the poet did at the flowers.

This is a March afternoon. It is a town school, Springfield. My group of keen writers and I have gone out onto the school playground. It is one of those unfortunate schools that hasn't a blade of grass to bless itself with, and so the old-fashioned word for playground, 'yard', seems all too appropriate. It's about sixty foot square and surrounded by twelve-foot high brick walls and a chain link fence which is presumably there to protect neighbouring gardens from footballs. There is no golden host here, just a few flowers lovingly planted in beds some six foot square. Someone has decorated the place with attempts at humanising it: hopscotch squares, circles on the wall to aim balls at, notices that suggest that children with no-one to play with should wait here.

It is not an inviting environment. But to anyone who is willing to look, being here has its pleasures. George Herbert wrote that whoever swept a room for 'God's cause' found 'that and th'action fine'. By analogy, anyone looking at anything with the spirit of exploration, with the spirit of finding some kind of truth, can expect some kind of blessing. One reason here and now is simply the surprise of both teaching and learning outside: this is a session in a course on writing, but we gather in the quadrant of a netball court under a sky mixed with bright and dark. We have no desks, but we do have notebooks. I ask the children to look at things hard, so hard that it begins to hurt. We study clouds. Someone notices, probably for the first time, that two clouds, one grey, the other white, in the same part of the sky, are moving at different speeds. Why should that be? I ask. There is no answer.

A few weeks later, I will show them images of cloud formations in books and on the Internet: cirrus – high, streaky, hair-like; stratus – spread out, flattened; cumulus – piled. Then they will be able to find the answers to questions like this: Why are some clouds streaky and thin, some fat? What dictates the colour of a cloud? I might even read them my poem, given at the beginning of this chapter, its first draft made alongside them.

Many adults who don't read poetry often think it has to be about the big guns – love, death, separation – while in fact it often begins with the smallest details. When I think about this, I often think of the paintings of Jan Vermeer – a woman in blue reading a letter, a girl with a pearl earring, a servant pouring milk with beautifully rendered bread, basket and blue cloth on the table. Dutch art is often made up of small things like this. And here are some lines by the priest-poet Gerard Hopkins, where he celebrates 'dappled things': 'rose-moles all in stipple upon trout that swim / . . . And all trades, their gear and tackle and trim.' As Dr Johnson is recorded by James Boswell as saying, 'There is nothing so little for such a little creature as man. It is by studying little things that we attain the great knowledge of having as little misery and as much happiness as possible.'

The French painter Camille Pissarro, quoted in Harry Mount's book *A Lust for Window Sills*, wrote somewhere 'Happy are those who see beauty in modest spots where others see nothing. Everything is beautiful, the whole secret lies in knowing how to interpret it.' See, for an example, my photograph 'When My Ship Comes In' in Chapter 4 (p 32).

Pissarro painted Norwood and other scenes of homely South London late in his life (he had to – he was fleeing from the Franco-Prussian War, which killed so many

Frenchmen and women), and this lends a kind of force to this idea. Some of these pictures are in the National Gallery in Trafalgar Square. He didn't need the garden of Monet, the Tahiti of Gauguin, the Opera of Renoir.

I ask the children to think of metaphors and similes, first for the clouds, and then for the many ordinary and familiar things around us – the litter bins, the six-sided tables with attached benches, the small troughs of flowers, the young daffodils, the fence, the brick walls and slate roofs of houses. There's forsythia shooting up in a neighbour's garden, only the top visible behind a wall.

The children have handsome hardback notebooks, bought especially for this course. I tell them to write 'rough notes' on the left hand side of a two-page spread. One girl writes her notes, starting with a cliché – though she doesn't know it, and it doesn't matter, because it is a springboard to fresher lines: 'Clouds like candy floss'.

I always mock, slightly, that cliché. Later in this project, children at the seaside will be challenged to come up with fresher similes, and they will surprise me. Here I let it be because this writer shows that she is looking; and also, it is worth remembering that it may not be a cliché to her:

Clouds like candy floss
snowy hill,
White on one side, dark blue on the other.
Dark like it's going to rain, but also sunny.

Forsythia – bright yellow like the sun. Spiky top.

Children rushing round then suddenly still and quiet. Ball making a rough sound as it scrapes along the ground.

Houses – symmetrical patterns, bricks in a pattern. Siren in the distance.

Sounds – crunching gravel on the road from car tyres. Helicopters.

Green bins like a mouth, beggar, smooth material, faded picture, you can hardly see it.

The daffodil middles are like yellow trumpets,
The ones that haven't bloomed are like green reeds.

The wind is cold on my skin, but the sun is so bright it makes me squint.

This is efficient note-making by a writer who is already practised in the important art of getting things down before you lose them. It doesn't matter, she has come to understand, whether your jottings are grammatically correct: what matters is that you have a record of what your senses have noticed, a record you will be able to use later to make something – a poem, a prose description, a letter to a friend, a setting for a story.

When I read my poems later, I notice this writer watching me and listening intently. I can sense that she wants to know what being a writer is, how you go about it. Some of the other children want this, too, and they show it in other ways. Since the course started a few weeks ago, several of them have brought in little booklets that they have made at home: A4 sheets divided into two and stapled together. They have put a title on the front, a contents list on the next page, and they are compiling groups of verses they have written at home. These verses bear no relation to what I am teaching – they are trite in subject matter, they often rhyme painfully – but they are evidence of a desire to 'be a writer', which is a powerful one, and one that I, as a teacher, have a duty to build on.

I am always pleased when children go beyond my lesson's aims. Here, with its pattern supplied by that repeated line 'On a March afternoon', is that writer's second draft:

> The clouds are like fluffy candy floss,
> Some white as snowy hills,
> Some as dark as blueberries,
> Though the sun is so bright it makes me squint
> On a March afternoon.
>
> Forsythia is in full bloom, yellow like the sun.
> Spiky branches stretch like skyscrapers.
> Helicopters overhead make a low humming noise
> Just like a busy bee
> On a March afternoon.
>
> Houses in symmetrical patterns
> Just like the bricks on the wall
> Though they sometimes have different shades.
> Children play with a ball, making lots of noise
> On a March afternoon.
>
> Crunching gravel on the road as the cars drive along,
> Sirens in the distance attracting lots of attention.
> A teacher tells the children to do better
> As the children have their PE lesson
> On a March afternoon.
>
> Green waste bins with holes like gaping mouths
> As if a green beggar man is asking for food.
> Faded pictures on the front, so pale you can hardly make them out.
> Smooth materials make it pleasant to touch
> On a March afternoon.
>
> The wind cuts on my skin like a knife
> Though the sun is softer
> Making it difficult to know whether to wear a coat or not
> So you just go back inside
> On a March afternoon.

Present participles, or what I call with the children '-ing verbs', are a constant problem in teaching writing in schools. Another writer in the group, for example, has written in her second draft, 'blasts of wind gushing past . . . chain link fences vibrating and rattling . . . vapour trails gradually fading away . . .'. Another has 'children speeding, dashing about . . . sun shining against the colourless ground . . .'. Both these lines have movement and vigour in them, but those qualities are weakened by the present participles. I have thought often about why children avoid main verbs in this way. Perhaps the participle form avoids commitment; is comfortably provisional. To use a blunt main verb makes something happen.

I took these two writers aside, and pointed out to them how much more muscular their writing would be like this:

> blasts of wind gush past . . . chain link fences vibrate and rattle . . . vapour trails gradually fade away . . . children speed and dash about . . . sun shines against the colourless ground . . .

Clichés, present participles . . . . Another problem with children writing is that they tend to over-write. This is not a serious concern for me: I suspect that every writer who becomes successful in writing the truth in a lively way begins with some going over the top. Indeed, it is important for me to remember the immediate thrill I sometimes feel from over-writing something until I realise, a few readings later, that over-writing was what it was, and I hit the earth with a bump. Here are two ten-year-olds from the Springfield group feeling that thrill:

> The deep dark nothingness of black clouds as everything disappears over the surface of the world . . . forsythia explodes . . .

> [a daffodil] is a grand king in an amazing turreted castle surrounded by guarding soldiers . . . it is a headache making siren . . .

Halfway through the session, I talked about clichés, banning 'trumpets' among other things, and collected similes and metaphors. 'What might you compare parts of the flower to? Think of things that aren't flowery . . . things that come from other parts of life.' Many fresh images emerged, among them these:

> Sealed up like peapods . . . pieces of butter . . . kings in turreted castles . . . yellow droplets hanging off green pencils . . . a witch's fingernails.

Later, the children research clouds and daffodils. One boy comes into school later in the course with a quotation that his mother had found in the 'Country Diary' of the *Guardian*. The trumpet that everyone associates with the flower is (he tells us) a 'freak of nature'. It's an 'elongated part of the flower called the hypanthium'. The apple (he expands) is the hypanthium of its tree, but in the daffodil, that organ makes this glorious shape, this trumpet, that lifts the hearts of many of us, that every spring shoots out at us. And, it is, we conclude, not quite as useful as the apple.

For the clouds, we found reproductions of Constable's pictures (see Barry Venning's book on Constable). The clouds in the famous *Hay Wain* picture (in the National Gallery in London), in his *Study of Cirrus Clouds* (in the Victoria and Albert Museum, also London) and in many other works will all stimulate children's thinking and writing – but preferably only after they have had firsthand experiences of cloud-studying.

Here is another group of gifted writers. The organising school is Aldwickbury Preparatory in Harpenden. Because the Headteacher and Governors are mindful of their commitments as a registered charity, the Head of English invites children from local state primaries to work in the school with me over a period of three days. The occasion is useful socially, not just educationally, as children who in the normal course of their lives would rarely if ever meet get to know each other and play together at breaktime. We are usually based in the Geography room, but this time we spend as much time as we can outside.

At this school, there is a yard much like Springfield's; but there are also acres and acres of grass – rugby pitches, fields, gardens, even some woodland. In the week following the lesson described above, I took a group of children out to explore a fine display of daffodils – not quite Wordsworth's host of ten thousand, but impressive. Among them were crocuses, and above the flowers a copse of deciduous and ever-green trees. This time I read the children Wordsworth's famous poem, first explaining 'jocund', 'pensive', 'vacant' and then 'gay' in its pristine sense (given in the *Shorter Oxford English Dictionary* as 'full of or disposed to joy and mirth; light-hearted, exuberantly cheerful, sportive, merry'). I also suggested that the end of the poem is much more than a pretty idea, that it encapsulates the poet's view of the relationship of humankind to Nature (which, I said, Wordsworth spelt with a capital N): 'And then my heart with pleasure fills / And dances with the daffodils.'

It was a cold morning with a slight threat of rain. Once more, I asked the children to make a page of notes while they were outside with the flowers. I hoped that the memory of my reading of the poem would still be fresh in their minds. Here is one boy's first draft:

> They are love itself.
> The stalk shows the connection to earth.
> The petals open out to show how free they are.
> They smell of the first angel.
> The bird song will always echo
> Near the pretty groups of daffodils.
> They group together like families.
> They scatter round the fresh green grass.
> The worms stay with them.
> They are a lovely thick yellow.

Then, back in the warmth of the building, he made his second draft:

> I could see a meadow of love.
> A place of utter silence.
> The only sound that was heard was

the echo of the song that the birds sang.
Their thick yellow colour shows how much these loving daffodils like to be
seen.
They group together in families of beauty and big packs of love.
They scatter around the fresh green grass.
They never complain about stormy weather.
They have come from the heavens, and been thrown upon us to show the
beauty of the world.
The petals open out to show their speciality of love.
The stalks grip into the earth to show their contribution of beauty to our world.

I am sure that the Wordsworth has made a contribution here. Even though this writer hasn't (how could he?) understood the poet's metaphysics, it seems to me as though he is determined to bring an other-worldly feel to his writing: 'They are love itself / The stalk shows the connection to earth' and 'They have come from the heavens, and been thrown upon us to show the beauty of the world.' Of course, these lines will strike an adult poetry reader as pretentious and sentimental. This boy has been seduced by a cultural definition of poetry as something that can only be about big things: a sure sign of that is the over-use of abstract nouns like 'love' and 'beauty'. The trowels and the spades and the digging and the sweat that went into making this display of flowers have no place in his poem, as they would in a poem by, say, Seamus Heaney.

But anyone writing under the influence of a Romantic poem for the first time would go over the top. And the words about the stalks' connection to the earth show how well Jacob has listened to me; and the words 'come from the heavens' echo, by dint of no more than good luck, of course (but don't all writers need some luck?), lines near the end of 'Intimations of Immortality': 'trailing clouds of glory do we come / From God, who is our home'. I was interested that the sentence 'They smell of the first angel' had been lost between drafts, and would have valued a chance to ask him why this had happened.

One further point about this boy's writing. We have reached a stage in the history of our society when it is, rightly, considered unjust to stereotype anyone in terms of sex, or sexual orientation, or race. In nurseries, girls are given as much opportunity to play with the building bricks as the boys; management posts in industry, at least in theory, are open to women (though they are paid less than men). Even if these assertions are over-optimistic, it is a fact that no-one could say in public that girls should only play with dolls and that women should expect to hold only lowly positions in industry. Or if someone did, there would be a hurricane of mocking laughter. But the image of the boy as someone who needs adventure stories to encourage his reading not only persists, the lack of them is being widely touted as a reason for their low test scores. This boy, like several of the others quoted in this book, belies this. His writing here, as I have already hinted, is if anything over-sensitive.

Of course, as one must, I had emphasised simile and metaphor, and another writer wrote:

Flowers of happiness in amongst the never-ending canopies
Make their own sunshine,

A tranquil meadow of joy
That dances on the darkest of days
Like a harmonious bright star in the night sky.
Nature's true beauty forms into one flower.
The daffodils expel the darkness,
Snowdrops look up at the king!

I had once again banned the word 'trumpet', because otherwise it is sure to figure too prominently in a class's writing on this subject: banning it forces the children to dig deeper in their imaginations for unusual comparisons. I had also warned the children against tired non-descriptive words about birds: 'tweeting prettily' and the like. I like to think that this worked – there were some examples of fresh writing: the trees (wrote someone) are 'like a cathedral bending over the world' and the sound of a bird is 'like a triangle'; another wrote about the birdsong 'like the sound of a flute'.

In the next example, a writer has built an extended metaphor into her strange fantasy, which I have reproduced exactly as I have it in front of me now on my desk. The question marks denote illegible words (I am using photocopies):

With light yellow heads and dark yellow mask
the daffodils go on the daffodil march
with shining green arms that sway in the wind
and a bent-down neck protecting the [?]
the daffodils go on the daffodil march

the birds sing like a subtle chainsaw
clover scatters on the ground and
the daffodils go on the daffodil march
soaring sky high lots of greeny brown
wait as the rain pounds on the branches
for something brown and still
the daffodils go on the daffodil march

wild bushes and different flowers sing
and dance for the sky is blue and the sun shines [?]
the daffodils go on the daffodil march

when the sun leaves and the clouds cover
the sky the daffodils bury their heads
and say goodbye
now all around is soft and quiet as
all the plants wait for the daffodil march

Strange indeed. But in children's writing strange is good, and always preferable to cliché.

Many years ago primary science was limited, almost exclusively in my experience, to sentimental 'nature study', and children were walked, in city schools, through local

29

parks or, if they were lucky, through woodland areas on one of London's many commons. I still remember the sudden surprise of a floor full of bluebells under tall trees, with sunlight shining through in great streaks. For many years they were, apart from daffodils, roses and tulips, the only flowers I could recognise with any certainty. In the classroom, we grew watercress on the windowsills. Now science is taught more methodically, but it is separated rigidly from the arts (as it always seems to be in the Anglophone imagination).

But all the writing quoted in this chapter contributes to science, because there is one activity that science, writing and art all have in common: observation. No-one can make a start on any of these studies at any level without committed looking. Accurate drawings of dissections, for example, have been crucial throughout history in anatomical education. A disease's symptoms have to be observed. Children looking at narcissi in one school began by restricting themselves to facts, but something kept creeping in. Just one example will serve here:

> The leaves come from the bottom of the flower. They are flat and long, and a dark green. Sometimes the flowers are yellow, sometimes they are white and they open out like a crown at the top. Sometimes the big petals are white and the little petals in the middle are yellow like the yolk of an egg.

This writer seems to be keeping to what he would consider the facts. He is reporting what he sees as though he were a Martian describing an earth plant in the manner of Craig Raine's poems, especially those in *A Martian Sends a Postcard Home*. The science is beginning in this bare description, but at the end he finds that he cannot do without a something more usually associated with the art of poetry – two similes: the crown and the yoke.

I began with catkins, snowdrops and daffodils. Each of the other seasons is open to this kind of close observational writing that can feed all kinds of learning. We just need to get the children out under the autumn trees, and then again when the black starkness of branches arrives and makes its shapes against winter skies.

4

In the town

1 High street

> He was a man who used to notice such things
> (Thomas Hardy, 'Afterwards')

Thomas Hardy was of course a countryman; and he meant in that poem a 'hedgehog travel[ling] furtively over the lawn, / . . . the full-starred heavens that winter sees' and the way the wind cuts a pause in the 'outrollings' of a funeral bell (his own funeral bell foretold, in fact). It seems unlikely that children now are taught to notice things like this, certainly not in the intense way that Hardy was taught, first by his family and then by himself. Life is too fast now, and multi-coloured in its imagery: the vividness of the screen makes the hedgehog and the night sky look monochromatic. A naturalist tells a story on Radio 4: he has seen a fox in his garden, so he calls up to his teenage daughter's room. She comes down, looks outside and says, 'And this should interest me – how?' Children, like all of us, have too much to notice. And certainly children are rarely taught to notice natural things in schools, where professionals are caught up in the trap of the numbers game, and where every conversation about learning is bleared and smeared with abbreviations like 'Sat' and 'Ofsted'.

I was a city child, and am a townsman, and I grew up ignorant of what Hardy knew. Twenty years ago, my knowledge of the countryside was random and sparse: oak, birch, cedar, yew, sycamore; wood pigeon, collared dove, blackbird, starling, thrush, tits (though which is which?), skylark, mallard, coot . . . a few more and that's about it. And although I have remedied some of this ignorance in recent years, most of my noticing is done with other things that my early schooling taught me to notice. I remember, for example, a teacher who helped me to examine poems: 'Look how the line "Generations have trod, have trod, have trod" *treads*!' said one teacher (the line is from Gerard Hopkins's poem 'God's Grandeur'); and I remember another who taught me to watch plays by taking me and other boys to see the very young Judi Dench in *Henry IV, Part 1* at the Old Vic Theatre; another (later) who taught me to look at pictures. He passed around reproductions to a group and suggested that each picture was saying more than we had thought. With its mixture of the holy and the erotic, Parmigianino's *Madonna with the Long Neck* was the turning point for me.

I remember those teachers for making me look in a way that, I am almost certain, children will not remember their teachers for, preparing them for their Sats. And, importantly, these passions have stayed with me. Poetry, drama, paintings. But this chapter is concerned with how, if we let them, everyday things can hold both our attention and also (and more importantly) the attention of children. Indeed, it is concerned with how looking at the ordinary can give a new dimension to our lives. Harry Mount has written in his recent book about architecture, *A Lust for Window Sills*, 'I get this joy from looking at buildings several times a day'. So do I. And I promise you that if you catch this bug you will never be bored in any town anywhere ever again. And I am not talking about grand houses and churches, but ordinary things. Window sills, bricks and gables, as Mount wittily demonstrates.

John Constable taught the English that the ordinary is beautiful. His *Hay Wain* (or *Landscape: Noon*) is often conventionally seen as an image of a lost past – a past that was, by implication, better than the present, a pastoral one, a past when life moved at a slower, a more human pace, as slow as a barge, a past when rustics had leisure. In fact the painting depicts a scene of contemporary rural poverty. And if it is still beautiful, this is not because Constable loved the poverty, but because he loved the bits and pieces that surrounded it: 'old rotten planks, slimy posts and brickwork'. The painter Camille Pissarro, quoted in Chapter 3 (p 21), echoed this conviction.

Much of what follows in this chapter is about finding beauty in places where the careless mind and the careless eye won't find it. Most recently I found and was delighted by a rotting boat (my 'ship') in Ipswich Docks.

My ship

A few yards from where I am writing is a small Victorian theatre. Inside it, I observe that it is almost square: today it would be labelled, euphemistically, 'intimate', while an honest word might be 'cramped'. Now the building is doing a different job, and if I were allowed to take the children inside it (I'm not: it's a pub) we could imagine the sounds, sights and smells of a Victorian music hall, and learn something about the fabric of life in both pre-twentieth-century days and in later days. I sit for ten minutes in the gallery (still there, with pub tables and chairs) opposite the place where the stage was, imagining the proscenium arch and the heavy curtains, and the applause and catcalls that must have greeted performers as they emerged from the cramped wings. Few people notice this building now, except as a pub. Neither do they notice the outdoor pulpit on a Methodist church, facing another street. I stand under it and imagine Victorian evangelists preaching. Nor do they notice the pigs – boars, really – that adorn many of the floor tiles in another church: the Victorian 'restorer' was a Mr Bacon – though some would use a less positive noun. 'Vandal', perhaps?

Somewhere along the line someone has failed these people who pass by these objects. It seems to me that a life lived without noticing – a hedgehog scuttling across a dark lawn, a full-starred sky, a poem, a play, a picture, the stage of a Victorian theatre – is a life lived missing something. And I believe that it is unjust that generation after generation is growing up damaged by a lack of looking.

A warm spring weekend morning, early. This is the only time when a modern Sunday resembles the ones I knew as a child. Those days – Sabbaths, really – were, as John Betjeman has written in his book *First and Last Loves*, the last visible traces of Protestant Britain: although religion had largely lost its grip on society, vestiges remained, especially on Sundays. Everything was closed, and families behind some of the windows would have been taking out their (what a dated phrase!) 'Sunday best' from drawers and wardrobes that smelt of mothballs. It feels a little like that this morning, and it would be only a mild surprise to hear someone practising scales or hymns on an out-of-tune piano. A child cries, not distressed, just wanting breakfast. A man sloshes soapy water over his Fiat Punto.

On this Sunday, it is safe to cross the smaller roads without looking right and left and right again, and the only mechanical sound is the occasional car ferrying a family out of town for a day beside the sea, twelve miles away. Even the local Fags, Mags and Booze Shop, with its mix of cigarettes, top shelf porn and strong liquor, all at bargain prices, is silent and boarded up with roller metal, and that shop hardly ever closes. St Matthew's has not yet pealed his bells. In this town centre almost every human being you see on a Sunday morning is alone, waiting outside a McDonalds or a Costa or a Caffè Nero, or wandering slowly along, and I always speculate on what they are doing, or what they are going to do; as they may do about me. One man is obviously on an errand to collect the Sunday papers and a carton of milk. A woman crouches to turn a pavement-level key to open a store that sells accessories.

And this is the best time to see my town centre and its architecture. About a hundred yards from my flat there's an alley. On the north side (my left) is a telephone exchange, and on the south (my right) there's St Matthew's Church. Anyone with the slightest knowledge of architecture could date roughly, if they looked, both of these buildings: the exchange, with its straight, clean, vertical and horizontal lines and right angles, and its concrete, rather shabby now, comes from the 1960s. There are other clues: there's no pitched roof, and the pale bricks contrast sharply with the flushwork (flint and stone) of the church which is obviously, even to the untrained eye, older; much older. To find out more will require some research, but its lack of round arches tells us that there is nothing visibly Norman (or, more correctly, Romanesque) here; that the church was built between *c*.1200 and *c*.1400; that generations of worshippers have seen additions and decorations to its fabric. From the west, where I have come from, I could see two huge side aisles, each one almost as large as a small church itself.

This church sends two messages: one says 'WHAT IS MISSING FROM CH—CH? UR!' on a notice board; the other is even more strongly put, though wordlessly, in the heavy chains and combination padlocks on the gates. Unlike almost all the other Anglican churches in town, this one, not just the building but the churchyard as well, is closed except for services.

So my epitaphs come from two other parishes near here where I often walk. There are so many lessons here: there's a rusted railing around a huge tomb about three by three by eight feet, with the same surname repeated many times over – here was a rich family in the nineteenth century, so sure of its status in the community that it spent money on commemorating itself. Odd, I always think, since they (presumably) believed that they were going to an infinitely greater glory, that they still needed this hunk of brick-built glory here. By contrast, here is an anonymous baby's grave from 1984: 'one of God's children'. And here is an explicit lesson for you and me – a grave with a verse:

In Memory of Samuel Ely
Who died 17 March 1820
Aged 37 years

All you who stop to read my stone
Consider how soon that I was gone
Both old and young a warning take
And mend your lives before it is too late

Children, like me, are fascinated by epitaphs on gravestones. I have worked with them in schools many times. In this verse, the faulty scansion and rhyme of the second couplet add a poignant note (as they often do). I stand by the grave thinking – as who would not, given the will to pause and a moment to reflect – a man young by the standard of our times, middle-aged by the standard of his; who is mourning him? Was he married? No wife has been buried near him, no children. Who paid for his burial? Who paid for this stone, and who wrote the verse engraved on it? Was it his elderly parents? Did he write it himself in repentance, like the prodigal son? How many have stood here in the intervening years, and taken that warning seriously? All these reflections will stir compassion in young writers, and provoke thinking and writing.

Another epitaph comes from a church in a village some fifteen miles away:

In Memory of
ELIZABETH HYAM,
of this Parish, for the

fourth time Widow;
who by a Fall, that
brought on a Mortification
was at last
hastened to her End,
on the 4th May 1748,
In her 113th Year.

That is worth my thinking about . . . but it is also worth children thinking about it.

Children do possess today, despite what might be supposed, a habit of looking. They have developed sensitive methods of examining everything the media presents, with such rapidity, to them. They interpret confidently what they see on screens, and the children in my group of keen writers, like other children, had pleasingly cynical reactions, pungently expressed, to many of the shows weekend television offers. The naturalist's daughter quoted above (p 31) may not have been interested in the fox in the garden, but there is little doubt that she was interested in and knowledgeable about the computer and television screens and the stories they were telling. What children lack is practice in looking at, and interpreting, what is still. Motionless. A Victorian theatre turned pub, a church, a grave, an epitaph. And children need to experience these, the primary sources of their own history or, if not that, the history of their own town. They need this experience, first because history is important; and second because looking intently is in itself valuable. When we look hard, we both think and feel with greater intensity. We are giving ourselves intellectual and emotional exercise.

The northern side of the churchyard in almost every medieval church is the left side as you face the altar in the east. This area has always been considered unlucky; it is not a coincidence that the Latin for 'left' is *sinister*. It is often home to an old yew and is consequently dark (the north-ness contributes to that too, of course) and in some places was traditionally used for the burials of suicides, criminals and unbaptised children. These facts open out to the children a fascinating area: the left-hand side is considered unlucky in many cultures. I have never explained this little group of facts to children on site without them going silent. It is a fruitful area for Internet exploration.

When I come to the end of the alley between the telephone exchange and the church, I have to cross a dual carriageway built in the sixties. You are supposed to step down into an underpass. But because there are no children and no traffic around, I run across, clambering over the central reservation. And here begins the main street of my town. Writing in his 1952 book, John Betjeman complained that 'when the suburbanite leaves Wembley for Wells he finds that the high street there is just like home'. In both places, wrote Betjeman, were 'Burton the Tailor of Taste, Hepworth, Halford, Stones, Woolworth & Co, Samuel, Bata, The Fifty Shilling Tailor, the Co-op'. I have printed that list here as a historic document: only two of those names – 'Burton' (though without its slogan) and 'the Co-op' – have survived the intervening sixty years, and that slogan, 'the Tailor of Taste', and that shop-front name, 'Fifty Shilling Tailor', seem as distant to us in culture as they are in time.

But 1952! What would Betjeman have said about this high street today in 2012? I walk past (I scribble in my notebook, much in the way that I encourage children to do) and note: Cancer Research, Shoe Zone, Showboat Amusements, Greggs Bakers,

Superdrug, Debenhams, an Oxfam shop, Help the Aged, Santander, Ann Summers and – a throwback – Moss Bros. Anyone who has the time and the inclination could write a historical and sociological study from those lists – I've even got a title: *Austerity: From The Fifty Shilling Tailor to Charity Shops and Shoe Zone*.

Our high streets are even more samey than they were in Betjeman's day. But all you have to do, he suggested in the 1950s, is to look up above the shops' facades where a higgledy-piggledy history of architecture is there in every city and town in England. Or you might just walk around with eyes open: either way, the sameyness is interesting. There's Exeter with its decorated cathedral next to a centre destroyed by an alliance of enemy bomber and sixties developer; there's Bath with its Georgian opulence; there's Chester, with its two street levels and Victorian black-beamed faux-Tudor; there's any new town – Stevenage, say – with its faded sixties socialist optimism gone to seed; there's St Albans, where in the high street you can see Victorian civic pride, thirties art-deco-and-water and sixties brutalism in a single glance (not to mention Roman bricks in the Norman tower of the Abbey).

A few weeks after my Sunday morning walk I took my Springfield group into town. As they walked, they looked and jotted, looked and jotted, as I had said they should. I pointed out that the Marks and Spencer building had the letters 'M & S' in stone high up. What did this tell us? There was much thought about this, and then someone said: 'It's been a Marks and Spencer since it was built.' I asked them: as we walk along, can we find other buildings that have probably been used for the same purpose since they were built? There weren't many. We stood outside a cinema, now a department store; a medieval church that was now a café; the theatre I've already mentioned, that was now a pub with just a nod to its old function in its name: The Rep. Even the W H Smith's store was identified as an ex-pub by one of the children: a carved stone sign high up said: 'CROWN AND ANCHOR'.

The children made their notes, but we didn't follow up the lesson with any formal writing as we did for almost every session in this book. There are normally two reasons why teachers expect some product, usually in writing, from children. The first and spurious reason is that if we don't extort something on paper from the children, we can't measure the learning, and unmeasured learning is barely worth anything. As the Headmaster, confronted by Hector's eccentric teaching, says plaintively in Alan Bennett's play *The History Boys*, 'How am I supposed to quantify that?' A soul-mate of his, an energetic and conscientious teacher, said to me this week, 'I am totally data driven': here was a teacher convinced that the Sats model served children's interests. In fact, the numbers game played so hard puts children's personalities so far in the long grass that they are forgotten. And balls through hoops – that is all that matters.

The better reason for expecting children to write is that they learn as they write. But even this reason is misplaced sometimes. I watched these children as they looked at 1930s buildings, and as they found others from the same decade; as they estimated where the town's edge was a hundred years ago by studying the dates of buildings marked in stone on the gables of the terraced houses where many of them lived; as they walked the narrow walkways, and thought about why they were so narrow (they are part of the medieval town plan); as they studied gravestones, and then the font and then the nave and then the altar in the church; as they watched passers-by. And I had to understand that they didn't need to write anything down. It was enough to look hard, and to be someone who didn't travel blindly though the world past the telephone exchange and the churches and the pubs and the shops and eventually, perhaps, the Eiffel Tower and Chartres Cathedral and the Pyramids and the Sphinx and the pictures in an art gallery and a comet in the night sky . . . but to be someone who, like Thomas Hardy, noticed things.

2 Football stadium

> The bits that don't follow the way it's spraying are like puffs of steam. Some water is going astray to where the clouds are high up in the sky.
>
> (Child writing at the Boleyn Ground, home of West Ham Football Club)

I've always liked football. This interest founders these days on news story after news story about the economic realities of the game. Players earn more in a day than a nurse earns in five years, and I think of that on every visit to my local hospital. Trading human beings for money struck me as barbaric when I was young, and still does. But that interest is still residually there. For me now, as for thousands of older men, it is a critical element in my relationship with my son, who has been coming to the same ground with me for twenty-odd years.

This primary school is some five minutes' walk from what is usually called Upton Park, the home of West Ham Football Club. I prefer to think of it as the Boleyn Ground, which is its real name. The area is dotted with the family name of Henry VIII's second wife: the Boleyn Arms on the corner of the road, for example, and a Boleyn café further down Green Street. It's an early summer morning, and a teacher, three Learning Support Assistants and I are escorting a group of twenty-five eight- and nine-year-olds through the busy traffic. We pass a statue of one of West Ham's most famous players, Bobby Moore, and three of his England teammates who won the World Cup in 1966. Next to the stadium is Our Lady of Compassion Roman Catholic Church. The parish priest and some of his congregation are standing chatting on the steps down to the street. All Asian, they silently refute a stereotype of the area.

We are met by members of the club's 'Learning Zone', who are responsible for outreach into the local community. The club colours, claret and blue, are on display everywhere in an extravagantly grand entrance hall. A princeling might appear at any moment in the shape of a player, but it is the close season, and none does. Behind the hall there is a warren of corridors with photographs of famous players from the earliest years of the twentieth century to the present day. The children, awed, walk past them silently.

The first adventure they experience, and the one that provokes the only really good writing, comes after leaving the players' dressing rooms. We travel along a short passageway, and then up more steps and . . . we step out into the stadium. I hear several 'Wow!'s. Much of the enthusiasm comes from girls; and not just girls, but Muslim girls, who, unless things change over the next few years, will not become fans – there are very few fans from the dominant groups in the local community. Now the children feel like players. We stand on the edge of the pitch, just in front of the dugouts. It is, for anyone who appreciates scale – that sudden jump from smallness to hugeness – or who has watched countless football matches, an awe-inspiring moment.

We look around, with our own imaginings. The empty stand opposite is silent, of course, except when those of us used to football grounds let our imaginations pretend that it's 3.00 pm on a winter Saturday. The children sit on the nearest row of terraced seats and I do my talk fast and urgently: 'Make sure you keep looking and writing your notes . . . remember what you know about similes – what do things look like, what do they resemble, what do they remind you of? And metaphors.' A huge water-sprinkler is working away. They jot notes, and later, back at school, they write them up:

> As I get ready for the greatest match I put my uniform on, I put my boots on. The net is ready to catch the ball. If I don't get ready fast enough I'll miss the match. The floodlights shine like suns in the sky. The water slices through the air like a chainsaw . . .

> The water reminds me of a waterfall
> with smoke spreading
> all over the place.
> The floodlights are as huge
> as a big button . . .

> There is beautiful green grass.
> There is no grass that is better.

This last simple statement must be seen against the background of a day at a school where there is no grass at all, and an area in which the grass in the local parks where this writer usually plays is rough, tussocky and meadow-like.

> The water spray looks like massive waves with white buzzing bees.
> The stand looks like files in a cabinet.
> The water looks like steam or smoke or mist or fog or a waterfall.

Both this piece and the next show something of what happens when young children – these are eight and nine – become habituated to thinking in similes and metaphors. These techniques, plus young writers' growing familiarity with them, and plus that quality all children have – a need to get things right – leads to vivid writing, like those 'massive waves with white buzzing bees' and these spraying puffs of steam:

> The water is like a water fountain spraying about. The bits that don't follow the way it's spraying are like puffs of steam. Some water is going astray to where the clouds are high up in the sky.

This piece is an example of a child wanting to get something exactly right. She has noticed what the others hadn't, and she has worked hard to find words for it. Hence 'bits that don't follow the way' and that use of 'astray'. In the first of those two pieces, that filing cabinet was a happy choice of phrase as well.

The water looks like smoke spinning around in circles floating . . .
The floodlights look like I am on a stage dancing . . . The water is like a huge
 tsunami . . . it makes me think of a train.

After the poetry of the pitch, with its potential for daydreams, and the water so
variously described by the children, the indoor parts of the tour were prose. We went
into the changing rooms. This next writer is working in her second language: see how
she relishes her skill in her relatively new tongue with her beautiful hyperboles, going
for a kind of poetry even in this prosy setting:

The changing rooms have lockers the colour of an ocean of sapphires, and
benches more red than a ruby . . .

All the children played the game I had suggested, thinking up similes for what they
saw. Some were not yet familiar with this idea; but they had begun to grasp it. This
was practice in using a technique that otherwise might merely be a classroom exercise.
On the other hand, similes weren't always appropriate to their subject – that is
evidence of how seriously the children take teaching, even when the results seem a
little odd: the bathroom is as white as snow . . . the blue lockers are coloured like the
sea . . . they are like mini wardrobes . . . the physio (originally 'fizzio' in nearly all the
writing) beds are like giant beds . . . the toilets are as peach as your skin . . . the massage
beds were brown like toffee . . . the benches are more red than rubies . . . the lockers
were the colour of sapphires . . . the sponge baths are more like a pool . . . they had
their own mini-fridge!
  This over-writing is entirely justified when you're learning about similes and your
teacher has talked incessantly about them; and, in any case, weak ones like those are
the price we pay for the vivid ones I've quoted above: the waterfall with smoke
spreading all over the place . . . massive waves with white buzzing bees . . . like steam
or smoke or mist or fog or a waterfall . . . puffs of steam . . . some water is going astray
. . . like smoke spinning around in circles floating. . . .
  One writer offered a summary:

The stadium is a beauty, packed with massage chairs, pools, and much more! I
went to the press lounge, all covered with sponsor badges including my favourite
SBOBET. Home changing rooms were fab. They had showers, lockers and their
own mini fridge, away changing rooms were different, they had no lockers, only
hooks. In the away changing room a big sign said THIS IS UPTON PARK
HOME OF THE HAMMERS.

The children learned some truths about football that they won't have learned from
television reports on games: that hospitality to away teams doesn't go so far as giving
them equal facilities in the dressing rooms – the away team have hooks, the home
team lockers, the away team have one physio couch plus a table, the home team have
two physio couches. In some grounds, architects, told that they must make the away
dressing rooms as unwelcoming as possible, design an L-shaped room, so that the
manager giving his talk before the game and at half time can't make eye contact with

all his players. They also learn how everyone is surrounded by rules: there are posters in the changing rooms banning jewellery, and elsewhere players are warned about wearing boots beyond certain points.

When I look over what the children wrote at West Ham I see it as the weakest material in this book. 'The waterfall with smoke spreading', 'the spraying puffs of steam', the 'white buzzing bees' and a few others all stand out among more ordinary sentences. This is, first, because I had no opportunity with these children to do what I call 'lighting up time' (which I will describe in Chapter 7): I met them cold just as we were about to leave the school. I didn't even know their names. Second, it seems obvious to me now that the setting of a football ground (especially in the close season) will always be less stimulating than an archaeological dig, or an art gallery, or the mixture of architectural styles to be seen on a walk down any high street. Those physio couches, those clothes hooks, that mini-fridge: these objects do not inspire (though the spraying water and the first sight of the stadium certainly did). They broke the rule about everyday objects always possessing their own beauty. Most importantly, this session was a one-off with these children. All the other groups represented in this book were familiar with me, and I with them. The best work will always come when a teacher or a writer has a twin commitment to children's learning and to words and all that they can do; and it will be all the stronger when the teacher or writer and the children know each other well.

And as I write (summer 2011) the newspapers are full of news about this part of London. The site of the 2012 Olympics, about a mile away, will 'regenerate' the area. This stadium will be razed, and its land will be regenerated or more likely redeveloped as flats. West Ham United will play, if all goes to plan, on the Olympic site.

3 The supermarket

> Learning through drawing prolongs the looking.
> (Mary Newland and Maurice Rubens)

Looking through a file of cuttings, I found that I'd published something about a project in which teachers and children from a school and an artist had worked together outside a classroom, twenty years ago. My first reaction was to stuff the notes and newsprint back in the file and to forget about that story. After all, in today's constantly changing educational marketplace little is worth noting unless early this morning there was a government initiative supporting it. And these children, I thought, with that distressing sense of time passing into eternity that, I suppose, all teachers have when such a thought occurs to them, are in their thirties now.

And then I took the notes and cuttings out again, and it dawned on me that, unlike government initiatives issued twenty years ago, this story was still alive. Yellow-edged the pages were, but the words on them rang true. I realized that I could take what I had written then and re-write it, first to build in recent thinking, and second to show that human activities done with a view to finding the truth outlast others done to suppress it. So I got my notes out again and added to them when (it was quite often) I noticed I had missed something; or cut something when I had written (also quite often) something dull. Or something pretentious. And the only datedness that emerged was in the fact that nearly every teacher would say today that there's 'no time for that sort of work anymore'.

Four-year-old James sits on the floor at Tesco's looking at several hundred bananas. Tongue out, mouth wide open, he plays with a big fat felt tip pen on strong white cardboard. Every sweeping curve forms the edge of a banana. Six quick strokes give three bananas joined at the top. Then big open strokes in circles produce a set of oranges. Other children brace clipboards against their stomachs with one hand. Their eyes are fixed on a bright display of apples reflected in a mirror behind them, and their pencils and felt tips move on the paper. There is a sense of play in their movements. Ordinary as the things around them are – bananas, apples, grapes in their cellophane packs, oranges – I am convinced about this for the thousandth time in my life as a teacher: drawing ordinary things not only makes you look better, it makes you think better too. I am convinced again that, as Mary Newland and Maurice Rubens put it in a booklet (I have done what I have always wanted to do, and played with their words by recasting them as a poem in free verse, or a set of aphorisms):

> Children who learn to look
> learn to question
> to discover
> and to understand.
>
> Learning through drawing
> prolongs the looking.
> Looking encourages concentration.
> Looking absorbs,
> engages,
> calms
> and sensitises the learner.
> Art is a way of looking,
> seeing,
> questioning
> and discovering.

There is looking, learning, questioning – and play – in all the children's work in the supermarket. There is also a sense of playfulness, too, in the artist's work. Dale Devereux Barker often experiments with pieces of card, many cut to a bottle shape, on tiny collages. Now he and these children are playing with images together. This is art out of the classroom and, quite literally, in the marketplace. Literally, because Barker has chosen this Tesco supermarket as a subject for his two-week residency with Tattingstone Primary School. He says to me later:

> I encourage the children to look more closely at familiar surroundings. It's not about photographic representation. It's a starting point where children can get fired. I'll try to guide and fuel their skills and their imagination. There is a place

for careful observational drawing, but art is for exploring, for trying things out
.... I want the children to play with abstract shapes, to look for balance in colour
and shapes. These children are not looking for exact likenesses, they are happy
playing with abstract shapes.

Dale, who is a tall man, crouches beside the small children. He understands (as many
adults don't) that it is important to be on the same physical level as young children to
communicate with them effectively. He is concerned not to make early judgments:

I do worry about imposing my values ... as soon as we start holding children's
pictures up we are saying what's good and what's bad. Trimming and mounting
children's work is mass editing. We don't like all that white paper, let's cut it off.
That's terrible, like listening to a symphony and saying, 'I like that bit, chuck out
the rest.' But the children know exactly where they want to things to go. The
white space around is important.

Dale begins to see the artist–child relationship from a different perspective as he talks
to the children; a perspective similar, perhaps, to the one teachers have, represented in
that mental file labelled 'The Things Children Say'. Dale suggests to one girl that she
should wash her hands. 'No, I want to keep them dirty. It shows I'm a real artist.'

On the first day of the residency, the children had visited Tesco to gather data for
the fortnight. They spread out around the store in groups of four or five, looking at
fish, tins, vegetables, and making line drawings of what they saw. But Dale had been
worried at first: 'They're not drawing quickly enough, they're too tight, we must
speed them up, move the groups quickly.'

Later he relaxes, impressed with what they can do in such a strange environment
... 'I couldn't do this with everyone looking at me.' The children draw without inhibitions. The drawings are like snapshots, done directly, recording the basic information they will need later. One nervous girl, only four years old, loses her worries in
her drawing, moving from wide-eyed and disoriented to confident and smiling during
the course of an hour's drawing.

The next day is the first day back in school. The room where the children work
looks as little like a classroom as possible. Part of an old school house, it is a bedroom,
probably, that has been transformed into an artist's studio, with a variety of these
objects: graphic tools, paper, and paints. The last are not just varied in colour, but in
type: ready-mixed, powder-based, even emulsion. And there are pastel crayons and
felt tip pens. Furniture has been arranged so that children can make choices about
how they will work – they can stand at an easel, perhaps, or, with large-scale work,
kneel or sit on the floor. Finished work hangs from a line across the room, ready to be
displayed.

Now, like a student on his first teaching practice, Dale has a cold. Then he says,
'Have you got any emulsion? I think we'll spread some of that about. Really loosen
them up. Big brushes.' Nearly everything he says is about loosening children, about
setting them free, about speed, about dumping inhibitions.

Even in a school as art-oriented as this one, there are problems circling around – a
difference between institutional values and artistic ones. Teachers have practical

problems that artists can largely ignore. Emulsion might stain the floor irrevocably, the cleaners might complain about the mess, Martin or Cheryl may well fall in the paint, some parents may not appreciate why the children are spending their time in a supermarket playing with art materials, what about (one is sure to say) the basics? Arthur has to go to see the psychologist.

Later, other differences between institution and artist will emerge: as he works, the artist is largely concerned with the process of play, the making of art. Examples of this abound in Sally Festing's biography of the sculptor Barbara Hepworth. When she is abroad being fêted after winning a major prize, she is aching to get back to her studio in Cornwall to carve; here, Dale celebrates continuing work with little if any thought for final products. The school, if it is any good (and Tattingstone is a marvellous school) feels something of this too – but the headteacher has other constraints, and also he feels a need for a product for governors, teachers, parents and children to look at later; if only to know for sure that something has been achieved.

There are other more dramatic differences between what a school values and what an artist does. One school presented a sculptor with the subject 'Royalty'. A class of children brought in, over a nine day period, objects that they associated with the subject: toys, royal wedding and coronation souvenirs, crowns, robes, press cuttings, pictures of Henry VIII and his wives and the like. They also wrote sentences, and painted and modelled objects that conveyed what they thought of the idea of royalty (or perhaps of a particular king or queen or princess or royal family). Between them, the artist and various children made a construction some nine feet high in the entrance hall of the school. They placed their found objects, poems, drawings and models on the structure.

A minority of these expressed negative views of kingship. Some of these expressions offended the school's values of respectability, which were, of course, bound up with other issues: the school's image in the local community, especially to prospective parents; order and discipline. Art has little time for this notion. It requires freedom, as these children need freedom in Tesco's. All art is exploration, about searching for a truth. The final product seems to be secondary to this first impulse, and Dale challenges the school's fetish about displaying on the walls. Dale only rounds things off because otherwise he wouldn't sell his work. Framing, he says, pays for his food. He relishes living on the line between order and chaos: that is not an option open to the school.

Later, in the studio, one wall is covered by emulsioned paper which, in turn, is being covered by a pattern of abstract shapes as small pieces of work are joined together. These are panels, each 30 centimetres by 20 centimetres, containing fish, crabs, fruit, vegetables and other images from the supermarket. Some other shapes have been gained by drawing round images previously drawn by children on an overhead projector and projected on the wall.

In the next room, children are sawing a large piece of hardboard into small squares. They are reluctant to stop, even when there are enough squares: the process again, rather than the product, is what matters; the learning that's going on, and the excitement of it, and the excitement of seeing their parts in the process making more sense when they are set among everybody else's.

5

Bringing something out of the earth

1 An adventure in garbology

What is so good about digging the earth?
You're on an adventure that no-one has thought of . . .

(Child's writing)

I tell them, it's been asleep for more than forty years, and now you've woken it up.

(Garbologist)

I remember watching my three-year-old son one spring morning over twenty-five years ago. He's squatting on his haunches outside a café where his parents are drinking coffee, and he's wiggling twigs or lolly sticks through the gaps in a drain cover. His friend, whose parents are also there and watching with interest, is directly opposite him, and he too is peering down the same drain. The crowns of the boys' heads are almost touching. What might be down there? Perhaps Daniel and Jamie are hoping to find some interesting living creature. Or some dead one. Or some mythical one – a troll from a storybook perhaps? Or perhaps the activity itself is enough. This lolly stick makes an interesting noise when I knock it against these bars. I can smell something. Can I see something shining? I'm glad Jamie's here too.

Either way, this pavement isn't, you might say, a proto-classroom. Daniel's parents haven't shown him this drain and suggested that he explore it; given him twigs and lolly sticks. Nobody is recording his activity. Neither is anyone monitoring his behaviour, though there will, of course, be a restraining 'Daniel . . .' if he pushes or shoves Jamie (very unlikely). But it is a place where he might learn something. Above all it is a place for wonder. And just because we parents have lost that sense of wonder in such things, such small, dark, dirty things, that does not mean that the sense of wonder these children feel is ridiculous; or in itself dirty.

And I remember him one winter. He was about the same age, but on his own this time (though one of his parents, his mother, was there). He'd been using a little plastic trowel and bucket to bring mud up the garden. He'd made a dam at the top of a little open tunnel alongside a stone stairway that linked the few square yards outside the house to the low lawn. As he came up the stairs from that lawn, he looked like a mini-ature Michelin man (I am looking at a photograph as I write). Fully protected by his mother against the cold and the wet – woolly-gloved, woolly-hatted, in bright yellow overalls – and mud-stained, he proudly showed me when I got home from work the results of his labour. But what I remember most is his wonder in the earth, and in particular his wonder in the effects of rainwater on it. Or, as a scientist would say, in the action of water on soil: what happens when a mixture is made of water and soil.

And I remember this: a Hertfordshire primary school some twenty years ago. I had asked children (as I often did, and still do): What are your six favourite words? One small, brown-haired child wrote down (I made a note) 'mud, dirt, worm, earth, goblin, dig'. Later in the evening she read her list to assembled parents, and I can see to this day her own parents' amused embarrassment. But (I could tell by their expres-sion) they recognised this earthy, wren-like, even mole-like, quality in their daughter, and for all I know one of them might have been remembering his or her own child-hood, and thinking 'That's my girl!'

Most children wonder about what they might find, given time and freedom from nervous, health-and-safety-conscious adults, in dark inaccessible places under pave-ments, down drains, in the earth. Where else do archaeologists come from, if not from that wonder? And where does that wonder become science? And where does the wonder go for everyone else? Have the artificial environments of classrooms got something to do with its loss? I asked one of my writing groups to remember when they were young, and what is was like to dig in the earth. They should find, I suggested, the most earthy-sounding words that they could think of.

The excitement is palpable for the first writer – that 'pitter-patter of your heartbeat // . . . on an adventure that no-one has thought of':

Dig, dig to the middle of the earth.
What will you find on your way?
The smell of the earth that's like a stony passage
and the feeling of crumbling darkness
also hearing the sound of slithering worms.

Dig, dig to the middle of the earth.
What is it like on your way?
The darkness is completely mad
and all you can hear in yourself
is the pitter-patter of your heartbeat.

Dig, dig to the middle of the earth.
What is so good about digging the earth?
You're on an adventure that no-one has thought of
from your fingertips to your palm,
that is something to be proud of.

Dig, dig to the middle of the earth.
How did you make it all the way?

With my own hands.
I feel triumphant because I found a treasure,
an emotion full of joy.

'Crumbling darkness' is terrific. The second writer catches a memory with a fresh simile in his first line, even an original one, and continues with an appropriate muddiness in his sounds:

> Crunch, the sound is like a person munching a stick of celery. Soggy earth splatters over my hands and drools off my fingers. Dry crumbling earth crackles as footsteps walk over it. Rubbery wellies trudge through the smudged wet mud. Gritty rain water trickles out of the lump of mud I grasp in my hand. The cracks in the dry earth are like spider webs and the tiny black ants scamper inside them.

The final piece shows an awareness of, and a skill with, words like 'bulky', 'toughening', 'blocks', 'drench', 'slop' and 'flop' that any many an older writer would be proud of. It also shows that urgency that children feel about getting things right, even the apparently most trivial:

> Your hands are covered in mud. It is hard and bulky. You can build a dam, toughening up the walls, adding big blocks of mud. Pour water on it again and again before it starts to harden and crack and crumble away. Parts start to break off and bash on the ground, getting caught up with the big waves in the water created by your fingers splashing about. But if you completely drench it with water it can slop and slowly flop down on the ground and collapse, causing the whole work of art to come to an end. And then when you get out your spade to get it out of the way, as soon as you stick it in, the water trickles out, bubbling, and rinses out of the mud.

All that comes from memories. First, my own of my son and his friend, and then of a girl in a school; and then children's, remembering under the stress that teaching can provide. The memories are mixed up with elements of craft – alliteration, and simile especially – and with another craft, that of the teacher; and in these days when many teachers have to behave much of the time as hired hands delivering a curriculum which they have had no part in making, it is all too easy to forget how powerful the teacher's craft can be if they are given freedom to be imaginative and creative. To turn that craft into an art, in fact. And how influential that craft, or that art, can be in the lives of children.

What about children working outside with the earth between their fingers? What if they studied garbology? William Rathje is an anthropologist who originated this study at the University of Arizona. He began to examine landfill sites with his students in the early seventies in the city of Tucson, and was able to show (among many other things) that residents of the city wasted ten per cent of the food that they had bought; and that the comfortably off wasted more than either the poor or the wealthy. Examining garbage bins produced reliable data about the population's consumption – more reliable, anyway, than the data that is usually gained from other sources, such as interviews. Face to face, people lie both to themselves and to interviewers; or at least they kid themselves about, for example, their consumption of alcohol. The harder, more reliable evidence, Rathje hypothesised, was under the ground.

He and his students dug up and then analysed the rubbish that households generated. This work led to innovative thinking about recycling, about what would rot away and become part of the earth, and what would not, what would instead be dumped in landfill sites for future generations to deal with, if they could. What he and his students learned had dozens of other practical uses – in education, for example, both in school and after school; in packaging, about how foods and other products are marketed. He was especially interested in the dietary habits of the poor, and his findings have had much to teach about education in nutrition and health education. His work is a classic example of how scientific method can document problems and identify possible solutions.

Rathje's work opened an avenue for children to explore what already interests them – even obsesses them – but which is rarely even thought about in classrooms: what is under the surface of the gardens, parks, fields, meadows and grass verges that they are so familiar with. Much of what they might find under these places would surprise them, and give them an insight into what the human race, with all its waste, is doing to the earth; an insight into what the world might become in a few generations unless we take giant steps to prevent global tragedy; and it helps them to see what small steps they as individuals might take.

I saw a few years ago two projects that capitalised on the interest children have in the earth and what is underneath it. The first involved the archaeological excavation of an icehouse at a local private school. Now I have to say that I didn't know what an icehouse was, so I asked the leader of the Suffolk Garbology Project, Duncan Allan (who had also equipped me with the facts about Rathje). He was the headteacher whose children we saw in Tesco's in Chapter 4, now free of that role. An icehouse, he told me, was a sort of eighteenth-century proto-refrigerator: an underground brick-built dome packed with ice and straw that provided a way of preserving food for the well off. At some point in the twentieth century this one had been broken into with a drain. It fell out of use and was filled with rubbish: material for young archaeologists to bring to light and wonder at.

Three agencies had come together to make this work possible: the Suffolk Garbology Project, led by Duncan himself; the Suffolk County Council Archaeological Service; and three schools – the host school, the local secondary and a special school. There were nearly 150 students. Outside their classrooms, students who in all likelihood would have had no interaction with each other were able to work together.

During the week, students, teachers and volunteers sieved the finds from the icehouse and found refuse from the school dormitories and classrooms. All this was securely datable to the 1960s. These finds gave the pupils an insight into life in a school with boarders fifty years ago. There were chunky little bottles of different inks, the very names – Quink and Stephens – redolent of that time; there were plastic protractors and the flat tin boxes that had contained them as well as other mathematical equipment, such as a pair of compasses, a six-inch ruler and the like. Some of this equipment had names scratched on. Graffiti on these and other items allowed present students to research their owners from school records. It was a simple matter to find the names in the school records and find out more about those individuals – possibly even to trace

47

them – and they could explore some of the differences between life in a residential school then and now. This was an unusual opportunity for students to work with primary sources. The children obtained an intense micro-view of a tiny part of the sixties through archaeology, and they were able to back their findings up later by looking at secondary sources – textbooks about the period, posters, DVDs, material downloaded from the Internet. They listened to contemporary recorded music, and talked with adults, parents, grandparents and older teachers about their memories of the period.

Another stage in the garbology project developed in surprising ways. Children in primary schools began excavations at a site by sieving out waste from earlier in the twentieth century. The finds were washed and set out methodically in 'find trays'. One aspect of archaeological practice was thus emphasised: how organised the work has to be. All types of domestic flotsam appeared: glass jars, bottles, shards of pottery, rusted tools, enamel advertisements for cigarettes and chocolate and other things. One of the latter was for a garage, and students were able to research it on the Internet. In a DVD made of the children working, one heavily gloved boy can be seen carefully scraping the dirt off a rusted hammer, another is lovingly scraping the outside of a pot and then probing inside it with the tip of a trowel. The camera watches this boy for some time in close-up, but he doesn't once look up at his friends or at the camera even for a second, so involved is he in his task. There are medicine bottles and flat jars that might have contained fish paste. There are examples of that object somehow representative of our times, the tablet blister pack. There is also, slightly shockingly, part of a set of dentures. All this gave the children something of a picture of life before World War 2; it also threw up many puzzles which would have to be researched later. But what emerges most from the film is enthusiasm: you feel it all the time as you watch the children working. And you can just catch a scrap of conversation between two children: 'What've you got?' 'I dunno, but it's cool.'

Some of the children invited older villagers into the school to help with research into the objects they had found. Slowly, in conversations with the villagers, and with handling of the objects, a picture of rural life came into focus, a life before mains water and power, a life until now unimaginable for these children. Other pupils visited modern landfill sites to compare them with the research site.

All this material led to writing . . .

Circles

We were interested in the past
    How people lived
How things were different
    We didn't want to waste
        What we had found
We wanted to make something from waste
We didn't want to waste our time either
We made circles because they represent
The life cycle and not wasting life
Circles are holes
We always imagine a hole to be a circle.

. . . and to art. There were collages, for example, made with detritus from the site, and close observational work in a variety of media; and some students worked in reconstructing, in drawings, the lost parts of pots and other objects. In the DVD, one child is copying a ceramic pattern very slowly and with great intensity. In another scene, two boys lean over a sieve that's resting on a red plastic box. It contains various finds, and the boys are beginning the evidently fascinating task of putting them into different categories. I notice that their heads are almost touching.

And then, more surprisingly perhaps, there was dance. At the time of this project (2009) the local authority employed a dance teacher, and Michael Platt worked in all the schools involved to help them to develop a dance piece based on the excavation and their impressions about waste practice. All the costumes were made from recycled materials. Through this medium, children were able to explore the stories of found objects: their useful lives, their being discarded; and through this to explore their own related emotions – How do they feel when they are useful? How would they feel if they were discarded? What would it be like to be lost underground and then brought out of the earth into the light? They were able to explore what was valuable; that it is not always the obvious – gold and jewels and the like – it is also objects that are, on the face of it, worth nothing, but which mean something in terms of memories: the children met older residents of the area who were able to make this point clearer. Other objects are precious in obscure ways: 'I dunno what it is, but it's cool.'

There was a performance at the town's New Wolsey Theatre which was filmed. Children from all the schools joined in this production, and at any one point there are some twenty or thirty children on the stage. The film is never less than absorbing viewing. As I watch it now, I notice how the camera's attention has been caught by one child. He cartwheels on from the right, then sits facing the direction he has come from, and slowly raises in turn each of his arms two or three times. Then he rolls over, repeats his action a little closer to us, stands, hugs his shoulders, jumps, hugs his shoulders again. Then he turns, his eyes intent on his raised hands, his 'focal point', which he then brings down to his body. All this takes about two minutes, and the child is both unselfconscious in the common sense of that word and yet utterly conscious of what his body is doing. And it is hard not to rejoice that this dancer is a boy. In one tableau, a mass of bodies gradually accumulates, presumably representing the earth. Plastic bottles emerge, held aloft by children whose faces I can't see: the bottles will survive.

Watching this film, I can see that these children have not been handpicked. Children with less fluency than others make their own statements: this is not an exercise only for 'gifted and talented' dancers. This point is relevant to the parts of this book where I have been working with children labelled as 'gifted' or 'talented' writers: other children could have benefited, as long as they were (my favoured word) 'keen'.

What follows are notes I made while watching Duncan Allan at work with young garbologists on another site in the Suffolk countryside.

> Ben, who is six years old, has found a shell, and he is cleaning it with an old toothbrush. Duncan asks him: 'What kind of shell is that?' 'An oyster?' suggests Ben. 'Yes. How do you think it got here? . . . Did it walk?' Ben thinks that it may have

been in a river and people collected it. 'Why do you think they collected it?' 'They were looking for pearls' says Ben, confidently.

He is one of thirty children from a nearby village primary school. Duncan has found in this Suffolk field a place for Ben and his classmates to study their families' own recent history, or at least the history of their grandparents' contemporaries. And his headteacher has had the wisdom to free these children from their classrooms for a day. Their work with Duncan will enable them to do what 'real' historians do: to find primary sources; to play with them; to examine them; to sort through them; to clean them; to categorise them; to talk about them; to write about them; to draw them.

'Real historians.' 'Real artists.' 'Real writers.' Children's experience of these three disciplines at its best gets as close as possible to what professionals experience. Children are not merely practising to be historians, artists, writers: when they work, they *are* historians, artists, writers. And to be practical, artist-children always have sketchbooks, and there is always a choice of art materials around them; there is always a proper space to enable them to make decisions about materials and how to use them. And, as no writer is ever without a notebook, the children always have notebooks; and those notebooks will be, if the children choose, private; and writer-children, like professional writers, need peace, so there are times in the school day when there is an intense silence wherever children are working. Inevitably, this will almost always be in a classroom. But archaeological sites, churches, art galleries, beaches – these places will all offer their own ways into silence. Clearer, surer, better ways. And into silences more intense. And no-one is a real historian unless she has experienced primary sources at first hand. To put it no more strongly, this is more likely to happen in settings like this than in the classroom.

Someone has to do some basic work before each garbology project starts. How does it happen? Duncan Allan said to me:

> We find a site where we know there's been a rubbish tip. We dig a test pit first to check for health and safety, and to check that there is stuff there. We use recent sites, from the past fifty years or so, first because with older ones children might destroy evidence – those places need experts – and also finds are limited. Here you find something in every bucketload, things they can relate to, toys, bits of cars, crockery, bottles. This site is mainly 1960s, and it's exciting for the children to bring something out of the earth. To clean it. I tell them, it's been asleep for more than forty years, and now you've woken it up.

Duncan imposes safety rules. There are gardening gloves for handling evidence, rubber ones for washing it. Then he says: 'There have been hundreds of children here recently.' Pausing, he looks around, making eye contact, it seems, with everyone. 'How many do you think have cut themselves on broken glass?' A boy responds immediately, thoughtlessly: 'A hundred?' 'No,' Duncan replies, and looks around the group of children. 'None?' suggests a less certain voice, a voice that is evidence that someone has taken a moment, just a moment, to think. 'Yes,' replies Duncan, 'none. And we are going to keep it that way.' 'Everything,' he says, 'is either a "nasty" or a "goody".' Nasties are dangerous things, like broken glass, knives, bottles that might contain dangerous fluids and the like. The children (wearing gloves of course) are taught to place these in a separate container.

Someone has found a fragment with 'Indian Tree' on it, and someone else a bottle that once contained Bouquet Dusting Powder. There is nothing as distant as the recent past, as these brand names make clear. Where, I wonder, are the Harpic tins of lavatory cleaner and the Double Diamond bottles and cans of my youth? Other finds are shards of crockery with a distinctive blue pattern that one child will recreate later with crayons, and which another, with two pieces, will proudly fit together in front of the camera, jigsaw-wise. There are dark green bottles that once contained, probably, medicines; rusted tools; coins; large shards of unglazed garden pots; nails; bones; and a tiny wheel on an axis with a handle, like those mini trundle wheels you use for slicing pizza. One find that interests me especially is part of a mug with 'HRH THE DUKE OF YORK' on the side, and above it the image of a man from his chest up to his thirties-style collar and tie: he's been beheaded! There is such excitement around, simply because every single object that the children bring out of the earth is a treasure.

After ten minutes, Ben is still cleaning his precious shell and telling his friend about his pearl hypothesis. Other children squat on tarpaulins, sieving the soil or digging about in it with trowels. Sorrel, seven, and Emily, six, have found a goody. It is the side of a pot, and Sorrel explains: 'It's got E-N-G on it! I bet that was England!' Two girls wait for Duncan to finish pouring soil into a wheelbarrow, barely able to contain themselves. What will they find?

There's an artist on the site, Clare Hamilton. She has her own marquee. 'We saw a rainbow on the way here, and I'm making a pot to put at the end of it. The children are going to make the treasure to put in it, or find it.' This comment shows something necessary in anyone working with children: an empathy with child-like minds that, in this tent, builds a bridge between this artist and that child-archaeologist carrying over, so tenderly, an unstoppered green bottle to put in Clare's pot; or that child who doesn't know what he's found, but who knows that it's cool.

For a break, the children crowd into Clare's marquee. It already contains objects made by children from a different school who had been working on the site. Junk musical instruments made from old bottles hang on a frame, and shoes made of clay, painted with natural pigments, lie in tidy piles on the floor: they had used shoes as a theme because they'd dug up examples by the dozens. The previous day, Duncan told me, there'd been a jam session, with Clare on recorder, a visitor on guitar and the children on 'junk percussion'. Now Clare, Duncan and the children discuss the progress they've all made filling in the pot at the end of the rainbow.

Later Duncan talks to the children, with seven-year-old Laura as an enthusiastic feed: 'What's in this pit?' 'Mud.' 'We call it soil.' Duncan explains that 'people threw stuff in pits like this one. They didn't have big landfill sites, like we do today. We'll find clues here, evidence for how people lived. We're going to dig it out.' When I leave, Ben is still thinking about oysters and pearls, and other children are handling evidence that will tell them something about the lives their grandparents, or even their great-grandparents, led.

2 The glow of the kiln in the woods

I like being here because it's real.

(Child's comment)

Though the garbology project had ended Duncan Allan went on working with young people in the authority's schools. Suffolk County Council's Archaeological Service secured lottery funding for a new project called *Unlocking the Potential: Exploring the Archaeology of Suffolk's Aggregate Landscapes*. The overall aim was (as the final report says) 'to explore the aggregates industry and the archaeology of the landscapes in which it works'.

Duncan Allan's professional background is in working with primary age children. He had been the headteacher in the village school that worked with Dale Devereux Barker in the supermarket in Chapter 4, and to say that the school developed under his leadership a high reputation, especially for the teaching of the arts, is to sell it and him short. The children often visited art galleries, and they were able to talk sensitively about recent painting. I remember listening to four or five 10-year-olds discussing Lucien Freud's *Girl with a White Dog*, a picture with a very limited colour range which depicts a semi-nude figure. They analysed it without any of the embarrassment that might have been expected, and were unfazed by its subject. The school hosted residences for painters and poets. And between two of the classrooms, Duncan installed a commissioned stained glass window with images of birdlife on the local reservoir. There was a rumour about at the time that he had spent the money on the window that he was supposed to have spent on the cabinets deemed necessary for filing Sats results.

Duncan's passion was (and is) with the spark that flies when and where children's learning and an artist's work meet. And while working in archaeology, the same model persists: he constantly has children's learning in his mind. The archaeologists' view of the work, on the other hand, was largely untouched by children and their intellectual needs. In an interview with Duncan, I had picked him up on one word that figures frequently in the reports: 'outreach'. In Duncan's words

Archaeologists are quite protective of their discipline, of their academic prowess . . . there's a little bit of academic snobbery there. It may be just through tradition, that they have not had a lot of contact with schools. But anyway a lot of their idea of outreach is working with history societies, giving talks, etc. While I believe, probably because of my background, my expertise is in working with young children . . . I see it in terms of its value for young children, using archaeology as a vehicle for outdoor education. I think that some of the officers see that as perhaps not being valid. Now my argument is, what is the point of archaeology if you are not passing it on to anybody else? It sits in a little box, as do most of our finds, they're locked up in warehouses and nobody sees them.

'As do most of our finds.' To work with primary sources; to work with the problems that the children's forebears faced; to learn about their history by handling their bottles, their tools, their dinner plates ... all this requires more, valuable as such activities are, than looking at museum cases and labels saying 'DO NOT TOUCH'.

The gap between the two views of what might be done with archaeology in an educational setting depends on different understandings of what a learner is. It is an old dichotomy that has been put in many ways: Is the learner passive and ignorant, sitting in a row listening to someone who knows? Or is she active in a laboratory or a studio or a seminar group? Has she got her ear clamped to one end of a speaking tube while someone calls out facts to her, or is she responsible for finding out things for herself, and interpreting new knowledge in terms of what she already knows? Is she a pot to be filled, or a fire to be set alight? In archaeological terms, is she looking at a pot in a museum case or is she getting her hands dirty at a site?

Whichever of these two views a teacher takes lies beneath everything she does, and influences strongly the way she teaches. Of course, it is not as cut and dried as that – there are times when the teacher who believes in the fire-to-be-set-alight model will behave like pot-to-be-filled teacher, often for reasons of safety – 'Leave the building silently and quickly without running,' says the first kind of teacher when the alarm goes off. And there will be occasions when the teacher simply tells children things: Duncan's words about 'nasties' are one example, as is his image of something being woken up when you bring it out of the earth.

Here are some active learners. In Tunstall forest in East Suffolk, Duncan is showing students how Celtic tribes made fire. We are all sitting in a circle with Duncan in the middle. Some of the students are from the top years of several primary schools and the others are from the first years of secondary schools. Duncan's flint works first time. He passes it around anti-clockwise, and when it comes to me, I burn my finger on it. He explains that nomadic Aboriginal tribes make fire this way today.

Duncan, he tells me later, is offering his students experience. He is not interested in supplying what he calls, witheringly, 'a drip feed of heritage'. He is presenting problems to volunteers and students that the Celts living in Britain would have faced in their struggle to survive: getting food (some of the students on one site trapped crayfish), collecting wood, making an axe, building a fire, cooking, weaving, clothing themselves. He is getting them to explore ways to solve problems. Much of this involves working with potentially dangerous tools. He makes an interesting point to me about safety: 'blunt knives are dangerous ... we work with sharp knives in good condition, knives that can do the job ... and we make sure the students know how to use them properly.'

That, he says, is about 'hard skills'. A list in a report on the work with these students and with others at different sites gives an idea of the variety of other such skills and related experiences that the study of archaeology offers. The students make pottery and spoons; they build structures, including a Roman-style kiln (and they fire it), a roundhouse, a clamp kiln, a shelter (and they sleep overnight in it), a smokehouse (and they test it); they process food and cook it, both meat and vegetables; they dye cloth from natural sources; they test whether a find was a sauna or cooking pit; they work with wood that they've gathered; and they knap flints ...

The work also helps with the development of what Duncan calls 'soft skills'. The report identifies them as: being able to communicate; being reliable; persevering;

The tepee in the forest

co-operating; evaluating information critically; taking responsibility; developing confidence; tolerating other students' and adults' views and their values. Many classrooms have posters on walls that represent attempts to get these points across. 'YOU'VE NEVER FAILED UNTIL YOU GIVE UP' is one example I saw recently. This is ignored by most students because they are not being treated as active learners but rather as an audience for platitudes. Here on the site these skills simply have to be learnt, or the job won't get done and there will be accidents. So they are learnt.

One of the principles that Duncan has established with the site is that each group leaves something potentially useful for the next. Already here is a Celtic roundhouse, an oven in which the students have been making bread. Duncan says to us all as we sit in a circle that the baking had been done 'by guesswork'. But the little loaf that emerges is, to judge from its appearance and the reactions round the circle from students who feel its crust and taste it, more than edible. Leaning against the oven is a wooden spade with a shaft about five feet long. It looks like one of the tools used by chefs in pizza restaurants. There's a tent-shaped structure made mostly of wicker-work that finishes a foot off the ground, supported by a dozen thin wooden legs. There are two human-sized figures made of wicker work, and piles of wood just gathered from the forest.

This book has many examples of young people's writing. But the comments that follow come from secondary school pupils talking about their camp later, to volunteers:

When I went there I was very quiet and found it difficult to talk to people . . . I didn't mix much. Since then I find it much easier. I talk to people and mix more easily. When I got home from the camp in September my mum kept trying to do things for me and I got really frustrated. I kept saying to her, 'Mum, I can do this myself!'

This is a moving document. This speaker, a girl in her early teens, knows something about herself that she not happy with (don't we all?); but she has felt able to express this awareness and her discomfort with it in speech to an adult. It seems likely that what she's experienced at the camp has helped her to be so frank, and that it has helped her in her everyday relations; in her confidence in herself. The last sentence is nothing if not a cry of rejoicing. And it is likely that experience gained in this environment will have a lasting effect.

The other piece provides evidence of benefits that are less tangible. There are memories of sensations, companionship and laughter that will stay forever:

I remember the silence of the night and how every sound seemed so loud. It's something we will never forget. We were sitting under the shelters and everyone else was around the kiln. It was very good having the glow of the kiln in the woods when everything else was so dark. It made you feel safe. But suddenly there was this horrible barking and we were so scared. It was Rob [the survival specialist]. He had crept up on us and was only a foot away. He had got so close and we didn't even know he was there. How did he do that?

The figures in the forest

Among other comments made by students on the sites, two matter especially to me. One said, 'I like being here because it's real.' Looking around it was easy to imagine what was in his mind. Because classrooms have been used as the default setting for learning since schools began, it is easy to forget that they are artificial: those shelves of identical reference books, the punctuation pyramid that everyone ignores, the list of names with varying numbers of stars after each one (everyone ignores that too). This student hadn't seen that artificiality. But he had seen the opposite. That human beings solving real problems, making bread, weaving, collecting wood . . . and just getting on under the Suffolk sky, had a kind of reality that his classroom hadn't.

Another student at the same camp said, 'I like it here, there is so much space.' This is another remark to make any teacher stop and think about the enclosed nature of classrooms; they typically contain so many humans in a small space. I remember asking a class of junior children about their favourite places in school, and one boy said, 'I like it under the stairs.' When I went to see where he meant, I found a large, dark, dusty space where it was quiet and where no-one else came. How often children must wish for more space.

A teacher on site had said to me, 'You don't have to tell a single child off!' Everyone knows that cramped quarters among animals lead to trouble; here, spacious quarters, and relaxed times, among other elements, had produced an environment that had a purpose, and which was peaceful, and which was a place where students could rejoice in self-discovery.

6

A day on Seaham Beach

I scraped a poem into a rock.

(A writer on Seaham Beach)

Someone – accounts vary, though I go for the 'sympathetic Scot' that the British composer Arnold Bax overheard – said that everyone should experience everything once 'excepting incest and folk-dancing'. (The reference is in *The Oxford Dictionary of Quotations*.) I watched folk-dancing one Saturday afternoon in Chester, and am glad to have experienced and indeed photographed it (though I was not invited to take part). My headmaster at grammar school said much the same thing as that Scotsman; though without, rather worryingly now I come to think about it, making the exceptions. Another headteacher (definitely not a head*master*) I knew much later, my friend the poet John Cotton, used to take the whole of his comprehensive school personnel – pupils, staff, cleaners, cooks, crossing patrol – to the local seaside town, Clacton, for a similar generic reason: it was, he said, an experience worth having.

The word 'seaside' has a particular resonance for members of an island race, although most of us are only occasionally aware of it. Many may well go abroad to foreign resorts every summer when they can afford it; but 'the miniature gaiety of seasides' (Philip Larkin's phrase in 'To the Sea') represents something tied in with childhood, and therefore with parents and grandparents, and children and grandchildren. Holidays have been recorded by Brownie box cameras, by twin-lens reflex cameras of enthusiastic parents, by camcorders, or by the multiple pictures taken today by mobile phones and digital cameras; but they have been enjoyed for a long time before that (think of the Victorians and their bathing machines – little huts wheeled down to the water's edge to preserve modesty) and they are enjoyed still. The seaside is central to our memories.

Someone told me once that the human race is attracted to the sea every summer – or at least to the safe fringes of it – because that great soup is the place out of which, millions of years ago, we, half fish, half land creature, crawled: so every human owns a racial memory of the sea as a universal mother. I once put this hypothesis to a friend. He looked at me scornfully, raised his face to the heavens, let fly with a sardonic hoot, and carried on digging a ditch in the beach for his children. He preferred a more homely explanation. Our childhoods, and memories of them: piers, promenades, slot machines, peep shows, deck chairs, sandcastles, crabs in beach pools, holiday camps – all that paraphernalia and more (he said) explains our nostalgia. But we live on a small island, and the sea would mean something different to us if we lived in a land-locked place like Shakespeare's Bohemia, which had no coast. It would have a different kind of mystery, unimaginable to us.

I asked some of my keen writers in Suffolk to remember their seaside holidays. One of them wrote:

> A lot of our holidays – seven in fact – have been at Cromer in Norfolk. We started going when I was three and my sister, Rachel, was one. I can remember most of them. We used to like going on the penny machines in the amusement arcade, and going on the pony rides near the beach. Those were the first times we stayed in chalets. Once we stayed in a fisherman's cottage, once we rented someone's cottage.

A teacher wrote:

> I remember guest houses where you had to go out of the house after breakfast and you were not allowed back till teatime. Which was the main meal. And if you had a bath it cost extra. And my dad took me down some mornings to a cafe on the sea front before breakfast and we drank tea as he liked it, the colour of brick, and that's how I like it now, how I've liked it ever since in fact, though without the sugar he liked. And I remember we weren't allowed to go in the amusement arcades – 'a waste of money' – and I remember rain more than sun, and I remember the pacamacs that I hated so much but which we were made to carry everywhere, wrapped up so they fitted in a pocket and I remember hiding from the rain in shelters along the sea front and how clammy the pacamacs were when you put them on, sticking to your arms.

Those memories were about Hastings in Sussex. Seaham is a small coastal town in Durham. It used to be a centre of the mining industry, but by 1992 all three of the pits had closed, and the town had suffered as all the ex-mining towns in County Durham and elsewhere have suffered: the mines were a large part of a town's reason for being, and unemployment was a blow at the self-esteem of everybody. It wasn't just financial livelihoods: whole swathes of the country were swept in the feeling 'They don't need us anymore.' Now, some twenty years on, even though cuts to public services bode ill for almost all of us, the town seems to be thriving in a new way. It is part of a heritage coast, and in the early years of this century the beach was completely cleaned.

As the coach carrying thirty children and a few adults from a village near Durham City drops into a stretch of road with a view of the North Sea, necks (including mine) crane: 'There's the sea!' We – teachers, student teachers, teaching assistants and I, the visiting writer – had brought a class of eleven-year-olds to Seaham. They came from two schools in another village that had also depended on what the mines had gener-ated: livelihoods and a sense of community. We were not there, perhaps unfortu-nately, as John Cotton's school students had been twenty-five years ago, simply to enjoy a day at the seaside: fish and chips, rock with the place name ingrained through it, candy floss, a walk along to the end of the pier, a go on the dodgems, cheap beer and pop (not that much of this is available at Seaham). We had our aim (though I didn't frame it like this until I started to write these words): it was to improve the children's writing through the medium of firsthand experience of an exciting out-of-classroom environment. The children represented, unlike most of the children quoted in this book, the full range of ability.

For the first half-hour after we climbed down from the coach we watched the harbour, one of the working parts of the town. A rough pyramid of rubble, much of it metallic and therefore catching the sunlight in little flashes; a crane grasping something in its claws and dropping it into the hold of a huge barge; a small lighthouse hooped in black and white at the entrance to the harbour; little hills of sand from which small, faint clouds drifted northwards toward Sunderland; waves hitting the harbour wall, at this distance, quite silently; and one of those bridges that lift a roadway to allow shipping through. As I type this now, it occurs to me that I did not see a single human being in the scene in front of us. Were computers, somewhere in an office, causing the arms of the cranes to swing and the claws to open? There must, I suppose, have been a man in the cab of the crane. Perhaps I didn't look hard enough.

Behind us a road droned, and on the other side of it there was a shopping mall built this century and named, after Seaham's connection with the poet, the Byron Centre. Later, for our break, we found ourselves among dozens of shoppers. As we approached the toilets, a man came towards us laughing and, hands raised making the surrender gesture: 'I give in! I give in!' Children outside their classrooms are an unusual sight, and worth a joke, worth unusual clowning behaviour.

We had reinforced the children's learning about metaphors and similes (it shows, as it showed in the writing in Chapter 4 about the Boleyn Ground, but at Seaham the figures of speech were stronger, more organic, rising naturally out of the subject matter). We had said that they could write what they wanted: poems, notes, reports about what they saw. They just had to look and write. They were familiar with the fact that, to begin with, they had to get their ideas down; they were not to worry at first about grammatical and spelling accuracy, or indeed whether they were (to use a children's phrase) 'making sense'. All that could come later. The same applied to any sketches they might make. This provisionality in first drafts is part of the currency of the school.

The children leant on the iron railing, stared and listened – and, equipped with clipboards and pencils, they began writing and drawing immediately, many of them filling A4 sheets in minutes. Some of the adults hovered behind them with fresh paper. What follows are some of their notes written on-site, and some of what they wrote a day later, when they were back in the classroom.

The first writer is not one of the most fluent. Next day, in the comparatively sterile quiet of the classroom, when we followed up these notes with the children and helped them to make second drafts, he delayed starting by ruling lines across the paper. Every writer has, I am sure, strategies for putting the substantive issue off when the white sheet of paper or the blank screen stares . . . I'll wash up the breakfast things. I'll vacuum the living room. I'll put the washing out. I'll check Outlook Express. This writer's strategy was to rule lines. There was a short one at the top, aligned centrally, and three others.

A poem from Seaham

His relative lack of fluency was shown in other ways: his handwriting was not joined up, and his sentences all ended quickly, as though they were short of breath. You felt when you read his work that he was indeed scratching on a hard surface. But he is able to surprise in his ninth line:

> The dust is like mist rising from the hills.
> The waves are crashing all around us.
> The ships are full of grit all over the place.
> The trash pile is shining in the sun.
> There's a lighthouse in the distance.
> The waves are sprinting.
> I scraped a poem into a rock.
> I can feel the texture of a rock rubbing against my hand.
> It sounded like the Dambusters' bombs when I threw the stones.

Another child wrote:

> There is a bridge that lifts up to let the boats in and out.
> The waves are crashing the harbour like a slap across the face.

Sometimes, the children hit on a structure that suited their subject in all its detail and variety:

> See! The cranes pick up the shimmering rubbish.
> See! The ships carry all the sand.
> See! The sand which has blown over like dust.
> See! The cranes crash together.
> See! The sun shimmers on the sea.
> See! In the distance there's a tiny lighthouse.
> See! The ships along the horizon.
> See! The flags going all around in the wind.
> See! The walls break down and erosion takes place.
> See! The different kinds of clouds in the sky.
> See! The waves crash together like they're having a fight.

Another piece is similar, though organised in a different way. It reads rather like a picture by one of the Brueghels – the Elder's *Children's Games*, perhaps, where you can see the bowling of hoops, the riding of barrels, the playing of leapfrog and many other games, some dangerous: where are those six ruffians going to throw that boy?; three boys are sitting astride a fence, trying to knock each other off; that barrel might break someone's leg. (This painting, by the way, which is in Vienna, is a powerful stimulus for descriptive writing.) In this writer's work too, so many things are going on, and the writer rushes to get everything down: 'rubbish . . . wind . . . sand . . . cranes . . . ruins . . . scaffolding . . . lighthouse' all appear in the first few lines. I was so impressed by the beginning of the second sentence, and after a while realised that it reminded me of a line in Ted Hughes' poem 'Wind': 'The wind flung a magpie away'. She has a writer's impulse:

> The rubbish shone in the sunlight, brighter than the sun. The wind threw the sand at the floor, and the cranes and the other machines screamed and screeched. The ruins that were old and decrepit had to have wooden scaffolding wrapped around them to support them. The lighthouse stood like a statue, watching every move that the sea made. A little dog trotted past followed by its owner. The sea danced in the sunlight. I can see a cargo ship asleep. The waves crash against the rocks. The rocks lie not moving at all. The grass and weeds that cling to the cliff sway in the wind. Far out in the distance I can see a boat that looks as small as an ant. The crane's claw clutched the sand and hauled it over and dropped it into a pile. I can smell the sea air. When I look up into the sky I can see the clouds sway in the wind. Grey, pale, white. There are streaks of them too. They hide the aeroplane that soars across the sky.

Another child wrote:

> The sea shimmers like glitter. The sun smiles down at the sea, and the lighthouse stands tall in the distance. Boats, as long as a giant's arm, are parked up. They are ready to supply goods over different countries. The sea slithers like a snake. The waves chop as they flow along. The harbour looks like a massive model. The rocks shine like stars and there are strings of seaweed. A boat called Karla C stands still as a statue. The sun shines in my eyes as well as on the sea shore. The distance of the lighthouse makes it look tiny, but really it isn't. A little black dog crawled beneath my feet. There is something green stuck on a rock, but I don't know what.
>
> The waves bob up and down like pendulums continuously. The curl of the wave is like an old man with a bad back. Seaweed slips and slides with its slimy skin and it dances elegantly within the sea. The industrial estate in the distance has a whole world of construction implements.

The whole scene did indeed remind one of a working model.

> The JCB looks like a huge yellow creature stalking around and scooping up loads of stuff with its huge black and yellow mouth. The sounds around me are: the sea coming up and up making the tide bigger and bigger, the little waves going up and back down, and all of the wind. Yet again the water splashed in my face.

Another child, a boy, wrote with a disarming delicacy only available to a young countryman:

> I threw a stone into the water. It made a cow dung sound.

There are so many neat inventions in all this writing: the poem scraped into a rock, the waves curling like an old man with a bad back, the waves like a slap across the face of the harbour, the sea dancing in the sunlight, and most of all, for me, that neat, unintended and precise oxymoron 'the shimmering rubbish'. Even the errors of judgment were understandable: the waves, for example, bobbing 'up and down like pendulums'.

Later the children wrote some haiku-like poems. Sometimes they drifted clear of this structure, and sometimes they were tempted by melodrama into writing lines that owed little to the setting ('Seagulls search for scrap' – but I loved this piece for its sheer eccentricity). Sometimes, their haiku developed into what might become the beginnings of adventure stories. The cloud simile in the one-liner was refreshing: an improvement on the usual variations on cotton wool, a comparison which once again I had banned. The exclamation marks on one title denote relief, I think: this poem was written by the boy who had scraped the poem on the rock at the beginning of this chapter.

> The ship battled
> the seas like a warrior in
> an epic battle.

The angry storm clouds
gather like my granddad
with the blues.

Clouds shaped like a poodle's face.

Seagulls search for scrap.
Cranes move like crabs catching fish.
It's a hungry boat arm!
It's a hungry boat arm!

The captain shouts Stop!
There is a boat over there, stop!
Stop! Stop! Stop! Right now!
Stop! Stop! Stop! Right now!

The ship is going to crash!

The wind makes the sand explode in the air.

Poem!!!

After tremendous tugging
At my broken brain
I finally dug up a metaphor!

(The original of this poem is shown on p 60.)

The sand drifts away.
Sea glistens like unseen pearls.
Wind tugs at my clothes.

The rubbish gleams under the sun like broken crystals. The sea looks like a soft blanket heaving about in the air shining in the sunlight. The sand blowing in the wind looks like a horror of fog arriving with a long lost ship. Something green and mysterious waits for the waves to carry it up and across the ocean. Is it seaweed? Is it a net? Or something else? Some dirty seaweed stays in one part of the sea and whooshes on top of the water. 1 ... 2 ... 3 ... waves on counting smash against a piece of rock.

To see how clever a piece of writing this is, one only has to recast it lightly, and there is the beginning of an adventure story:

The rubbish gleams under the sun like broken crystals. The sea looks like a soft blanket. It heaves about in the air, shining in the sunlight, while the sand that blows in the wind looks like a horror of fog arriving with a long lost ship. Something green and mysterious waits for the waves to carry it up and across the ocean. Is it seaweed? Is it a net? Or something else? Some dirty seaweed stays in one part of the sea and whooshes on top of the water. She stands on the cliff top and stares down: 1 . . . 2 . . . 3 . . . . She counts waves as they smash against the rocks.

I have made this revision; this could have been made better by the writer with some teaching, but there was no time.

Not only was there writing to do but the children were making sketches. They didn't have available the variety or indeed the quality of materials that they would have found in a few classrooms – the staff had brought along the basics: pencils, paper and clipboards. But, leaning on the rails, they made drawings in between making their notes: the little black-and-white hooped lighthouse, the bridge that lifts up and, later, the JCB. Some even made sketches of the waves crashing against the shore. The teachers had not brought erasers. We felt that rubbing lines out, whether they are the lines in a drawing or in a sentence, is a waste of time, and that there is always a risk that you might lose something that you might want later. And in drawing, the 'wrong' lines are often interesting in the final product.

I remember when I began to understand something of how the act of drawing feeds into the act of writing, and *vice versa*. Page after page of Leonardo's *Notebooks* is covered with exploratory writing and drawing of all kinds of things, artificial and natural. I leaf through reproductions of them now (see A E Popham's book, *The Drawings of Leonardo da Vinci*), and choose at random: a water pump, a dredger, a snorkel, a flying machine, cogwheels and gearwheels . . . . Or I find cross-sections of branches, copses leaning in the wind and plants. Or I find a foetus, a liver, a spleen, an alimentary tract, the muscles of the upper arm, the actions of a man mounting a step and the 'hydrostatics of the bladder'. There is a relentless, restless mental energy, a desperation to know. There is an underlying understanding that it is possible to get things wrong, and that to get things wrong is a seriously bad thing. It looks like the work of a superman.

But that energy in Leonardo's drawings is akin to the primal urge of a child. My year-old grandson plays with a new toy. He can't draw it, of course. He can't write about it either. He can't even talk about it – at least not in words that his parents can understand. But he wants to know what it will do. His concentration is as intense as Leonardo's was. How does it work? What will it do? He stares at it, and at his hands as they manipulate it. He wants (and here is where he and Leonardo come close) to understand it. To get it right.

And Leonardo's work was done – where? The notebooks suggest that it was done in mechanics' workshops, in studios, in mortuaries or from the artist's imagination. In any case, the children were learning in a similar way as they drew in the supermarket in Chapter 4, and so are these children as they draw and write about what they find on the seafront at Seaham.

Later, we went to a part of the beach where there was no work going on except by a man in a JCB moving up the sand, making a U-turn, and then moving down again toward the tide. Walking down from the promenade to the beach, a group of us discussed what he might be doing, but we could discern no purpose in his actions. A few people were walking dogs that skipped in the soft waves, and swam in their ungainly manner; otherwise the beach was empty except for our cheerful group. Sunderland in the north was visible in the shape of a few metal silos.

The idea here was first simply to play, as one should on beaches, with pebbles, sand, seaweed – and each other; and then to write: to play with words. George Byron had married a local landowner's daughter (disastrously as it turned out) and he was mostly bored here; but he had watched the sea we were watching 'in all the glories of surf and foam'. The children unknowingly followed in his footsteps, and came up with some unhackneyed turns of phrase: 'the sea shuffling', for example, and that 'blue and white portal' (though I admit here that the handwriting, further obscured by photocopying, is not reliable). The streaky clouds 'like brushed hair' is perfect, and later I find out in *Encyclopaedia Britannica* that these clouds – cirrus – are described as resembling locks of hair, tufts of horsehair, a bird's tuft. Three of the pieces are accounts of another session with the student artist, when everyone collaborated to make images of sea creatures from pebbles and seaweed.

The sea waves dance their waves to the shore.
As the froth glides across the sea top
Twirling waves crawl through the sea.
The sea shuffles on to the shore then slides back.

The waves dance when the wind blows. The boats bop up and down on the sea. The sea fights the rocks to reach the wall.

When I look up at the sky, it looks like a blue and white portal [?] that goes on and on as if forever.

The clouds are so different, there are streaky clouds that look like hair that has just been brushed, there are fluffy clouds that look like a blanket that's just been fluffed up for a good night's sleep, and there are splattered grey clouds that remind me of a naughty child painting on their bedroom wall.

'Go, go, go' shouted Miss Whetton as we stood around the outline of the jelly fish. We scurried off, scavenging [this girl has written 'scouraging'] the beach for dark grey or black rocks. We needed these because Miss Whetton wanted the outline of the jelly fish to be dark.

Every time we brought back a huge or unique rock, Miss Whetton would say, 'Wow!' or 'Oh yeah, that's lovely!' After about ten minutes, the main part of the jelly fish's head started to take shape. Personally, I thought it looked brilliant, and everyone agreed too.

Louise found some glitter. I mean, who would have thought you would find glitter on a beach?

After the head was completed, Mr Walker and some other people started filling in the tentacles with pebbles. Once they had been filled in, we started to collect red stones – these were for the lips.

A sigh of relief came from everyone's mouth once the challenge was completed. We all stood back and looked at the masterpiece. The lips were vivid red and the eyes stole the show. We were so totally going to win! [They were in competition with the boys' creation.]

Becki, Shannon and Annabel collected lots of stones in Annabel's coat which helped us to gather them together quicker. When we had added the finishing touches to the jelly fish, we had to write this story that I am writing now.

I was making notes while the children were building their sea creatures. Writers in residence are not only with children to teach them to write in the obvious way, but, if it's possible to find moments, to write themselves; to teach, in fact, by example. So I sat on one of the low walls that led from the promenade to the sea's edge and made notes. When I got home I tried to make my notes into a poem:

On Seaham Beach
Summer 2011
(to the children at the Sherburn schools)

We made a flat jelly fish with rough pebbles and slimy seaweed today.

And while we're asleep
  in the dark
   the tide will come
    creeping like a dream
     to wash our great flat jelly fish
away.

More of the children's writing:

A JCB attacked the sand by scooping up rocks and sand. The horizon stayed away, avoiding us. Its secrets still untold! The sea flowed, throwing itself off the sand, creating splashes on the way. The city through the distance looked like a tiny model with miniature figures as people. I found a pebble with intertwined patterns. I threw it into the sea with great power.

If you lie down you can see the clouds. They float in different shapes and it feels as if they are about to drop on you! The seagulls squawk as they swoop down.

Umbrellas not needed at our beach.
Nauseous people come away from the sea.

I had anticipated someone would make the first comparison in this next piece:

The lighthouse is black and white like Newcastle colours. The clouds are like elegant swans. They are like unravelled balls of string. They are like giant air balloons, slowly moving in. They spread out like melting butter. The foam in the sea is a meringue mixture. Horns blow like vuvuzelas. The sea acts like an angry teacher telling a naughty pupil off. Eroding rocks, leading to a smaller population in the world. Luckily, it will take hundreds of years.

Sexual chauvinism is inevitable in primary schools:

> The black grubbiness in the sea makes the waves look dark and dirty. All the girls scream and wail like maniacs. Pebbles crack and crunch under my feet.
> The boys are like investigation dogs sniffing around after clues. They look a bit weak to carry the stones.

Back at school, I read some of the children 'maggie and milly and molly and may' by e e cummings (who doesn't use capitals much – neither in his name nor in most of his poems). Everyone who goes to the sea, he suggests, brings back something of herself. maggie's shell takes her troubles away, milly makes a friend, molly discovers her darker side; while may comes home 'with a smooth round stone / as small as a world and as large as alone' (cummings' poem is widely published – I'm using Michael Harrison and Christopher Stuart-Clark's anthology *The New Dragon Book of Verse*). The poem is a little spell, an enchantment, and if you read it like that, obeying the almost totally absent punctuation, children feel its magic and write *their* magic:

> My brother went to the big big sea
> And brought back something curved and red
> And he said to me
> Take this, it is my heart.
>
> My brother went down to the sea
> And brought back a white feather that was clean with no sand on.
>
> My mum went down to the sea one day
> And brought back a sweet wrapper
> But in the sweet wrapper
> There was no trace of sweets!

The next writer wanted to get just about everyone she knew in her writing. Nova was a member of the staff at the school who was leaving that day. She had just come into the space where we were working bearing gifts – sweets for everyone. Some of these lines are very sensitive, especially the last one about Ryan:

> Nova went down to the sea one day and brought back
>   a sweet stone to show how sweet she is.
> Joel went down to the sea one day and brought back
>   a booming shell to show how noisy he is.
> My Dad went down to the sea one day and brought back
>   a stone to show how generous he is.
> My Mum went down to the sea one day and brought back
>   a souvenir for everyone to keep forever and ever.

My sister Verona went down to the sea one day and
    brought back some fish and chips for everyone
    to show how kind she is.
My brother Ryan went down to the sea one day and
    brought back one dull stone and one colourful stone
    to show how he is feeling.

Tired, on the bus travelling back to school, from clambering up and down rocks and stone stairs, and from teaching under the influence of ozone, I reflected what a classroom we had spent the day in. The ceiling had been a sky that shifted colour by the half-hour, at one point gleaming bright, at another glowering, and at another sending us scurrying for paltry shelter under the promenade. On the beach, we had all found treasures: stones, seaweed, glitter. We had got to know each other better, too, seeing each other out of school clothes, and with hair whipped up into strange shapes; hearing laughter that could only be called, in the old-fashioned sense of the word, gay. And one of us at least (and I don't mean me) had scraped a poem onto a rock.

7

In the gallery

I detest a day of no work, no music, no poetry.

(Barbara Hepworth, *A Pictorial Autobiography*)

1 Making a gallery

[E]very child at play behaves like a creative writer, in that he creates a world of his own or, rather, rearranges the things of his world in a new way which pleases him.

(Sigmund Freud)

This project began when 20 nine- and ten-year-olds from Bealings Primary School, just outside Ipswich in Suffolk, went on a study trip to St Ives on the north Cornwall coast. I didn't go with them, but I researched their work for an article. They had stayed in a hotel a few yards from the sculptor Barbara Hepworth's house with its studio and garden. When they got back to Suffolk, they made sculptures in the little garden at their school. I talked to the headteacher and his colleagues; most of all I spoke to the children, and saw what they made when they got back to school.

The project's aims had been threefold: to study the work in the nearby Tate Gallery, the work of the local painter Alfred Wallis and the garden and studio of Barbara Hepworth. But the garden had entranced everyone so much that it took over. I had visited the Hepworth studio and garden some years before, and I'm looking at a photograph on the back cover of Marion Whybrow's *Portrait of an Art Colony*. The smooth abstract sculptures seem to grow out of the grass, and they suggest, with their roundness and their holes, the strength of stones, of the pebbles on the beach. The place abounds with shrubs that I'm too ignorant to name. Some soar like green fireworks, others hang, others provide a lush covering out of which the art reaches. In the picture there are four daffodils.

It is a kind of paradox that, even though they are abstract, these sculptures (like everything that Hepworth made) celebrate humanity. This is first because, if any observer looks with care, he or she will sense the human hands that smoothed and worked on rough surfaces to make them calm and smooth; second because the scale of each sculpture honours in some way the dimensions of the human body; third because the shapes remind us of the pebbles we picked, collected and threw when we were children. And there must be other reasons . . . . Perhaps one is that the trees and shrubs make the place an open room with, on a fine summer's day, a blue true dream of sky as its ceiling: a room where, if the world was new, some of us might choose to live.

In St Ives, the children explored Hepworth's work. One wrote later:

> The garden has lots of wonderful sculptures . . . they all have holes in them! It is a wonderful place . . . the workshop is full of hammers and statues that aren't finished . . . her overalls are still hanging up.

Like the poet Gerard Hopkins the children were drawn not just to the work, and not just to the artist, but to the tools that the hands had used to carve – in the poet's words the 'gear and tackle and trim' ('Pied Beauty'). Other poets have celebrated implements. See, for example, Seamus Heaney's dedicatory poem to his book *North*: that 'helmeted pump'; that 'slung bucket'; and, most of all, that 'tinsmith's scoop / sunk past its gleam / in the meal-bin' (from 'Sunlight'). Tools like this resonate throughout his poems – 'A latch, a door-bar, forged tongs and a grate' from the poem 'Lightening' in the 'Squarings' sequence in *Seeing Things* is typical of the sense of the home, the hearth that he achieves. Such words, or at least 'their' things – those hammers and overalls – meant much to these children.

They sat in the garden and looked and sketched from different angles. Adults and pupils touched the sculptures – a necessary privilege with statues, I would say, but one usually denied (for good reasons, I know) in conventional galleries. They also photographed them.

Back in Suffolk, and set alight by their experiences in Cornwall, the children played. Nothing is more important to a child, apart from the experiences of love and loss, than this activity, and they play, if allowed, about those subjects too. As Freud wrote, 'every child at play behaves like a creative writer, in that he creates a world of his own or, rather, rearranges the things of his world in a new way which pleases him.' These children manipulated materials, they put things in their chosen order, and they made believe they were great artists. This book is based in part on the fact that children are, if they are allowed, constantly at play with their environments.

They made clay models of the sculptures, and painted pictures of them. They began to plan their own sculptures and their own garden. They sketched and made clay maquettes. They made armatures from steel rods, hoops and chicken wire. They covered them with Modroc and cement render. Finally, they painted and varnished the sculptures. 'My favourite bit. The painting!' wrote one child. 'We put on loads of layers of paint and mixed lots of colours. Then we varnished them. We will have bronze and silver sculptures which won't get battered by the weather.'

But the Hepworth-style pieces have weathered, and here and there, as the Modroc decays, the insides are exposed: ribs of wire mesh, plastic hoops. They have a crumbly look. This only increases the interest of them, for the same reason that the outdoor sculptures at Grizedale (see the 1991 book edited by Bill Grant and Paul Harris) become even more interesting as the weather joins in the art-making and deals with the pieces, eroding edges, rusting steel, colouring them white with snow, melting them, covering them briefly in autumn leaves, making them shiny in rain. Or look at the way the interest of my boat (pictured in Chapter 4) increases as it disintegrates . . . at least to me.

The children have made other works of art and now have their own gallery in the small school garden. When I photograph them early in the autumn during their morning break, they are sitting in the yurt they'd made with the help of a storyteller. 'It's a dome . . . you can make it with anything . . . . It was used by the Mongols of Central Asia . . . . The wood might eventually collapse, but the plants growing over it will keep the shape . . . .' They peep through their own pastiches of Hepworth's work. They hide behind trees and bushes, reminding me of T S Eliot's line in 'Burnt Norton' about the leaves being full of children (from *Four Quartets*). They play with structures made of scrap material. The most striking of these is a rearing horse constructed, with the help of a local artist, from rubbish thrown out by the landlord of the pub at the bottom of the road. It's built from, among other things, a wine rack, a rake, a barbecue grill, a section of fencing, a hosepipe, wires joined together . . . . 'They wouldn't let us have the toilet!' One of the children tells me that the horse 'comes from that war picture by Picasso' and two other children chorus, '*Guernica!*'

There's a totem pole, over twelve feet high, with a grasshopper, a spider and an ant crawling on it. This was built, like the yurt, with the help of storyteller Paul Jackson, and the children enthusiastically tell me his story: all the animals tried to put the sun back in the sky, but only the spider could manage it. The children are delighted to see a real spider in its web between the one they had made and the pole. There's a little tunnel made of wood, like the yurt, and a rough gate at the end, and some tiles, made of pebbles, glass, clothes pegs and other detritus, based on themes from the Cornish artist Alfred Wallis. The children had enjoyed his work in St Ives. The gate's there, the children tell me, because the reception children kept running through the tunnel, 'and it wasn't safe'.

The children gather in groups over the little pool as children have gathered around water since the dawn of humanity. This one is based on Monet's *Waterlily Pond, Green Harmony*. They watch and play with an intensity that adults would do well to remember and emulate. Or they simply play, running about in a frantic game of hide and seek. Some of them make memorable little models for life studies, sitting on benches reading alone or to each other, peering through the pastiche Hepworths, examining the materials on the metal horse, looking into the yurt from the outside, or crowding inside, like students used to do in telephone boxes. The art they live amongst will be a rich soil for the future.

Art is the most powerful way that humans and children make can sense of the world they live in. Societies without art, or with art that is prescribed by the government, are soulless, dangerous places. I think of Stalin sending the great poet Osip Mandelstam to his death in the Siberian salt mines because he wrote a poem making fun of the dictator's moustache: 'art', as Shakespeare writes in Sonnet 66, is so often 'made tongue-tied by authority'. I think of Hitler banning Mendelssohn's music because the composer was born Jewish. And I think of the dreary, ominous official art that both Fascism and Communism produced, all muscular young men and women facing the sun and reaching out bravely to the future, with not a whiff of a human being about them – or at least, not a whiff of a humane being, which is much the same thing.

Neither pupils nor teachers had worked on such a large scale before, nor had they worked with sculpture. Pam Fletcher, the teacher, told me how the children's focus shifted; how they concentrated; how they learned away from their classroom:

> They modified initial plans as they came across constraints and new possibilities. They worked with tenacity and concentration, even when things did not go to plan. They were highly motivated and, finally, proud of their achievements. They were able to make large 3D images, and then set them into the school's environment. The children now have a love of sculpture, and now there exists a lasting resource, for the school and the village . . .

The headteacher Duncan Bathgate told me: 'The whole project had involved decision-making as the children's learning became more and more self-directed.' As the arts educator Robin Tanner said, 'The arts above all other activities involve us in the subtle element of choice. Every creative act is an act of choosing' (quoted in Morgan 1988). When I look back at this project, I see choices being offered and made almost all the time, and that makes it infinitely more educational than the limited training that is offered by the National Curriculum and 'delivered' exclusively in the classroom.

Studying children in an art gallery educates the attentive teacher: children are open to new experiences, and this includes art that adults find 'obscure' or, in that modern weasel word, 'challenging'. The children at Bealings seem to have no problem trying to understand and to enjoy modern art. Many adults look at non-figurative sculpture and turn away baffled: I remember a friend stepping inside the west (liturgically, that is; geographically, it's the north) door of Coventry Cathedral. There, of course, was Graham Sutherland's enormous tapestry *Christ in Glory* dominating the church from the east (geographically south) end. She said: 'I don't like that.' No child would be capable of such a peremptory dismissal. Children readily take up the challenge because they are untramelled by the notion that art has to be photographic in character. There are further examples of this in Chapter 8, when another group of children visit the Sainsbury Centre in Norwich.

A new group of children will work in this area next summer, using the garden as preparatory work for the next visit to St Ives. That group will bring back responses, and so the garden will grow in unexpected ways. What Duncan calls this 'echoing back and forth between the two gardens' is central to the life of the project. There's also an echoing between different classes of children. There's another hint of this in Chapter 5, where children working on archaeological sites use structures that other groups have built, and make new structures that will in turn be used by other groups: a practical recycling of materials, skills and emotional responses.

A storyteller . . . a local artist. Now that I re-read it, these two phrases jump out of that account. And it occurs to me that, even if some of us find it difficult to get children out of their schools very often, we can at least get something of the life outside the school into it. The presence in a school of anyone not immediately concerned with schooling – an electrician fixing a computer, a police officer talking about safety, a mayor showing off his robes and chain – all these can and usually do bring a welcome sense of the outside world. Storytellers, artists, theatre groups and visiting poets (I declare an interest here, as I have been practising as the last for many years) make a unique contribution, because they bring into school gifts that all the children are working on day by day.

2 A Suffolk gallery

There is the shape of five dancing dolphins,
a young man falling off his red surf board.

Bright roads leading through darkness . . .
(Children's writing)

This redbrick building stands about two hundred yards from Ipswich's main street. To get to it on foot, you have to cross a dual carriageway – it's one of those parts of town friendlier to motorists than to walkers. It stands in the inappropriately named 'High Street', which runs at a right angle northwards from the real main road, and, unlike any other high street I have known, is shopless. The largest buildings house dentists (three of them), the Oddfellows Hall, an independent pub named after the local arboretum, a 'will shop' and the town's Victorian museum. Some are still houses, and some of these have been converted into flats.

There is also this redbrick 1930s building, with bright pink signs up, repeating several times that this is the Ipswich Art School Gallery, open every day except Sunday and Monday, admission free. It used to be part of the Ipswich Art School. It's octagonal inside, with two floors, and rooms off each one – presumably originally teaching rooms – slightly odd-shaped to make the building four-square in appearance from the street. The art school has an illustrious history, and for the last few weeks the gallery has been displaying work by a range of artists with various connections to it. The art is arranged both around the lower and upper rooms, and also in some of the little rooms off them. Some of the artists were tutors, some were students. Edwin Thomas Johns (1862–1947) is represented here by a sentimental watercolour of a woman sewing, called *Memories*. This picture's presence is explained by the fact that he was the architect of the building. There is a notable contrast between the building's sturdy functionality and the painting's tweeness. There are watercolours by a well-known Suffolk painter, Leonard Squirrel (1893–1979), who lovingly depicted many local scenes; and there is work by current students on the BA course at University Campus Suffolk.

I have brought my Wednesday afternoon children here. It's that group from earlier in this book – they appeared in Chapters 2, 3 and 4 – seventeen eight- to ten-year-olds whom the teachers at Springfield school have recognised as 'gifted'. We have got to know each other well. Normally, a typical afternoon begins in a classroom with poems – typically, but by no means exclusively, Charles Causley's, my own, other contemporaries', Shakespeare's, Thomas Hood's, lots from Anon. Then there's what I think of as a 'lighting up time' to kick start some prose or a poem; sometimes, in the middle of the afternoon, there's a brief session with some numbers games to change gear, or there's a run on the playground and a deep breath or two to keep us alert. Finally, there's a coda with some more verse from the oral tradition – counting out rhymes, clapping rhymes and the like. This is rather tidy account of what actually happens; but no afternoon goes by without poetry.

This one is different, though. When we arrive at the Art School, now a gallery, the children are faced (as I had told them they would be) by a large canvas of about two metres in length by one high, by the artist Maggi Hambling. Depicting a wave breaking, it is directly opposite the entrance. Hambling had been a student at Ipswich Art School, and she is famed in her home county for many reasons, but especially because of her marvellous sculpture *Scallop*, a memorial to Benjamin Britten, set magnificently on the beach at Aldeburgh, with its haunting lines inscribed along its top edge, the outer, serrated part of the shell. They are a quotation from Montagu Slater's libretto for Britten's opera *Peter Grimes*: 'I HEAR THOSE VOICES THAT WILL NOT BE DROWNED.'

The children stare, obviously impressed, at *April Wave Breaking*. I ask questions, trying to make them as open-ended as I can: questions that do not lead to just one 'right' answer, but which (I hope) might lead to different possibilities and make the children think. I also make suggestions for techniques that they might use in their note-taking:

What sounds can you hear in this picture? (I am always struck that children are never disbelieving of this, on the face of it, odd assertion.)

What colours are there in this work that surprise you? And why do you think they are there?

Look in your minds for similes and metaphors that might help your writing.

What shapes can you see in the painting? Use what you know of maths.

How do you think the artist has made what you are looking at?

Don't worry about getting your ideas down in any 'perfect' way. Just get them down – but make sure that you and I can read them later.

What follows is: the titles of the pieces the children chose to focus on; the artist's name; a brief description of the piece (in italics); and what some of the children wrote while they were in the gallery. Later they had opportunities to make their notes into prose or poems.

Maggi Hambling, *April Wave Breaking*, 2002

This picture, about 2.5 m by 2 m, shows one huge wave as it crashes in front of a contrastingly plain pale grey sky. It is the kind of painting that will engage anyone's attention, and I wouldn't

Scallop by Maggi Hambling

want to spend much time with any adult who doesn't 'get it'; I knew the children would give it their attention immediately and freely. The paint has been applied, it seems to me, in many different ways, not just with brushes. I point out to the children that waves have insides, and that the insides of this wave are in the very centre of the construction.

Navy gold blue and white. Colourful red, grey black and yellow. You can hear the sea whistling as the wave comes down. Shadows and reflections everywhere. They are under the wave and on top of it. They are crashing loudly as they hit, splashing up and coming back down. As the sun reflects, it drops so loud you can hear it miles away. She's splatted all the paint to look like the sea.

This child is playing excitedly with words. So are the rest of the children quoted here.

Crash
curvy
floaty
waves
Red because of blood of killed animal
yellow because of sun reflection
bridge
circles
bird – seagull
slopes
water-fall

swerving
roller
half-potato

Waves crashing against the shore low   whistling.
Red – the fish that have gone too near the shore
Yellow – the sun on the waves
White sea-foam looks like the lid of a chest.
Circles
swirls
like a giant mouth
eating everything in its path
a sponge
a roller
a brush
her finger

Here is that old problem that's come up before in these pages – the 'ing' word, in this case a present participle. Later I will point out to this writer how much more dramatic his first line would be if it began 'Waves crash against the shore . . .' and then I will go further by suggesting that the line is a cliché. Could he think of a fresher word than 'crash' in this context?

Another child wrote:

The sound of the wave is like a huge elephant jumping in the water.
There are splodges and splats of colour like red yellow and brown.
The ocean splashes in the air and looks like a graceful dolphin.
She has probably used her hands and fingers.

And another:

Blue – shell as the eye of the sun.
There is the shape of five dancing dolphins,
a young man falling off his red surf board.

Note to this writer (never sent): 'This is beautiful and strange: "five dancing dolphins . . ."? And I love your first line, partly because I don't quite understand it. In your last line, would "A young man falls . . ." be better?' I remember steeling myself to face up to the challenge of explaining why the 'ing' word in the penultimate line (again a present participle) was fine, while the one in the last wasn't. The reason is that 'dancing' is acting as an adjective, while 'falling' is a verb that hasn't made up its mind.

Dark inside wave
hillsides
sponges
smooth lines

Waves look like eye brows
Inside you would see circles and even semi circles.
The wave reminded me of birds flying in the air.

Crashing like thunder
splats of blue
dots of yellow like sand dashing from wave to wave.
Hemi spheres curling round
Shapes and colours bursting up in the sky like the shapes of flowers
Inside a wave is a neverending tornado.

Again, 'burst' would give the penultimate line such muscle. In fact, this writer re-drafted this piece quickly to see what it would be like if she followed my suggestion:

Crash like thunder
splats of blue
dots of yellow like sand dash from wave to wave.
Hemispheres curl round
Shapes and colours burst up in the sky like the shapes of flowers
Inside a wave is a neverending tornado.

In these little pages of notes, the children have come up with several arresting similes and metaphors: 'the lid of a chest . . . a giant mouth . . . a huge elephant . . . a graceful dolphin . . . five dancing dolphins . . . eyebrows . . . birds flying . . . shapes of flowers . . . a tornado'. I'm sure that 'half-potato' has a place in there, even if I can't see it.

Maggi Hambling, *Wave Tunnel*, 2010

Hambling made this bronze some eight years after the painting, and it is obviously a development from it; or, you might say, a later part of her learning process about the sea in Suffolk, and how she might explore that obsession, playing with different materials. Indeed, she made a monotype, Wave Curling, in 2008 that was presumably part of her preparations for the big painting, as well as being part of that learning process. That monotype is also displayed here. The bronze is shaped like a huge brandy snap, or an empty ice cream cone with part of the cone shape missing.

Bumpy splashes from here and there, inside it's rough too. Bronze all over it. It looks so life like, like it's really there!

Swirls in getting wider
Curves inwards

The curling wave looks like a massive bronze shell.
Inside it is as dark as a panda's skin.

I wonder where that panda's skin came from. It's not nearly as puzzling, though, as that half-potato earlier. When children write comparisons that we as adults can't understand, we should give them the benefit of the doubt. After all, verse that gives up all its meaning has its home on a Clinton's greeting card, not in a book of poems.

> Dribbling sea splashing
> Like the eye of a hurricane
> white for the splash

This note is developed, with the same first line, in the postscript at the end of this chapter, on p 83.

The phrase 'eye of a hurricane', cliché though it may be, is hard for most adults to visualise. Here this writer has, unconsciously, taken the phrase and rinsed it clean. After revisiting the gallery and looking again at the Hambling and giving it further thought, I realised that she is trying to make an image in words of the hole at the smaller end of the bronze. She is the same writer who wrote about 'the eye of the sun' in response to *April Wave Breaking*.

> Bumps like hills.
> Bronze like a penny.
> Curls going up and down
> Black and white.
> As vibrant as the sun
> Red orange and yellow like fire bursting
>
> Waves running down like tears on a face.

'That is beautiful,' I said to this writer, and wondered, Where did these tears come from? This note is developed, with the opening 'This wave is sad' in the postscript to this chapter (p 83).

Maggi Hambling, *Rosie the Rhino*, 1963

This ink drawing dates from Hambling's student days at the college that used to inhabit this building. Next door is the town museum, and there Rosie the stuffed rhino has greeted visitors for many years. She is depicted by Hambling in close-up, charging at the viewer, and strong, controlled circular lines of varying width drawn round the outside of the animal's head serve to emphasise her power.

> Black and white
> strong back
> horn as hard as a rock
> skin as rough as a brick wall
> squinting eyes
> bulging tummy
> soft upper lip
> slow plodding feet

pricked ears
humped back
rounded bottom
scraping ground ready to charge while grunting.

Strong horn like a knife
ears quick and sharp
squinting eyes
strong mouth

This note is developed, with the first line 'Black and white', in the postscript to this chapter (p 84).

I had talked about the Hambling sea pieces, *April Wave Breaking* and *Wave Tunnel*, before our visit. These two and *Rosie the Rhino* cried out 'Look at me!' and the children did. The next picture had a similar effect.

Brian Whelan, *Transmetropolitan*, 2010, oil

This enormous piece is upstairs in one of the small rooms off the octagon, and is about 3 metres by 2.5 metres. Although it was described as being an oil painting, there are scraps of silver paper and advertisements, often Irish in character – St Bridget's Finest Porter, for example – but the background is London. So Foster's Brewery is there as well, and London underground trains and buses. It is, at least partially, a collage, a medium that most children are familiar with, if only superficially. Whelan has described this work, which he has made in nine sections, as 'a joyride across the city'; but it has tragic as well as joyous elements. It is visionary, and uses images from Christianity, and in particular a Roman Catholic version of it. A worried Noah sets the dove free; the frightened disciples let down the net. There is a graveyard, there is a skeleton (both of which immediately attract the children). There isn't (despite that word 'joyride') a face that you could even describe as cheerful. But it is exhilarating! The whole construction is held together by lines: an underground train swoops into and through a flaming Hades, a flyover flies above and hell's flames flicker around it.

Transmetropolitan is a huge presence in a small room, and I felt a little sorry for the other artists represented in the same space. I was so pleased to hear the intakes of breath from the children: their enthusiasm is palpable in what they wrote:

> There are a lot of different colours. Red, greens, yellow and blues. There are trains and buses everywhere. You can see signs for food. There are churches, graveyards, dying people. Floating boats and a plane in the sky. The little children from school in the graveyard. Skeletons and skulls are dotted around the place. Tiny little stairs and bricks around.

This note is developed into the poem with the first line 'There are lots of different colours' in the postscript on p 84.

Skeletons and lots of skulls . . . ZOMBIES!!!
Red dragon eating Jesus and disciples.

Kids in graveyard.
Robbers, man and woman.
Lady playing fiddle.
Church lamp posts
flying ark and a fishing boat
red buses
steep stair cases
train red as blood
fire, bursting flames like colourful tongues sticking out from everywhere!

Shiny tin foil
Very noisy
Dark colours
Beer
Lots of red
Different colours, planes

Zombies
Tin foil
Lots of beer
Lots of scenes
Lots of buildings
Lots of red and orange
Lots of cars
A grave yard
A dragon

     Aeroplanes
Trains driving everywhere.
     Praying
Bright colours standing out.
Street lamps
Skeletons lying around.
Different shades of blue for sky
London bus (London Pride)
   Fire orange red
Spooky graveyards
Fullers
Church
People dead
Guinness
Irish shop
Green grass
Lots of red in sky
Fishermen
Bones

Trees
Materials and stickers and bits out of magazines
Everything outlined in black

These last three children often begin with lists like this in their writing, and then fail to go beyond this technique. I pointed this out to them, and suggested that they develop their writing more.

Ray Exworth, *Man Swinging a Boy*, 1955, bronze

This bronze is about 50 cm high, and depicts a father leaning back swinging around a boy, who is stretched out horizontally. There is a powerful feeling of father–child love.

I can look at a piece like this and admire much of what the artist does with technique and structure. And I don't play that down: I visit galleries whenever I can to develop my understanding of art, what I loosely define as the mental side of things. But this piece (as thousands of others) moves me as someone who looks at art and sees sparks fly from that work to central parts of a life I've lived and am living: as a son of a father long gone who (or so my memory tells me) never played games like that with me; as a father; and now as a grandfather. And it moved this next writer who, it turned out, misses her father: he (she told me) doesn't live at home. She is the writer of the note 'Waves running down like tears on a face' and its subsequent development (p 83).

Happy faces are all around
Every detail exact
The boy is bouncing in the air
Like the man is about to fall down
If they were moving
Maybe doing it in mud squelch squelch squelch
Standing in a big muddy footprint
Wind swaying to the left due to a
Windy hair style

Guy Eves, *Tulip 'Stresa'*, pencil

This small drawing is made with scientific exactness, but it drew from this writer a lovely metaphor – those 'Bright roads lead[ing] through darkness.' She seems to have a sixth sense for metaphor, and she often doesn't need to go through the simile stage:

Buds ready to burst
leaves drip drop like rain
I imagine them to be pink (the flowers)
Bright roads lead through darkness
(on the leaves)
Buds to burst in a second or two

There are two major advantages that teaching about art in a gallery has over teaching about art in a classroom. First, in the classroom, only the teacher teaches. In the gallery the art teaches. The teacher – in this case me – has so much less to do, so much less pedagogical energy to expend, because the art is doing the hardest and by far the most important work. Of course, there's been the children's teachers' teaching of the whole curriculum over two or three years; of course, there's been my teaching of writing over the last two months; and there's been my preparation of the children for what they will see for a day or two. And there is the usual emotional energy to expend on teaching – increased something like tenfold by the emotional energy that looking at art requires.

But, once we entered the gallery, Maggi Hambling's *April Wave Breaking* was the real teacher. It did so much by its sheer presence on a wall, so much that a teacher conventionally does. It had class control. It gripped the children's attention. It made them quiet (not that these children were making much noise as they came into the gallery). But, once it had done that, it began to put ideas into their heads and, as they went on looking, it continued to put more ideas in, and to help them to develop the first ideas. Or more exactly *April Wave Breaking* in its medium set the children free to develop their own ideas in another medium – words. The process was fast, and not just with this painting. The gap between one girl's first sighting of the tulip drawing and her writing 'Bright roads lead through darkness' was no more than ten minutes.

The second advantage of teaching and learning in a gallery is that the children are looking at real art: surfaces a sculptor has smoothed, brushstrokes the artist has made. Children are seeing art at full strength; they are not seeing it in the watered down form in which they usually see it – in reproductions. (That is, of course, assuming they see it at all.) To walk round a gallery is wearying because we are encountering artists' attempts to come to terms with their experiences of living on this earth. This involves intellectual and emotional engagement, neither of which comes cheap. Reproductions, necessary as they are, have several disadvantages. We can take them or leave them with a turn of the page, or with a shuffle of the postcards. They draw nothing from us. We don't even have to walk past them.

And their size: I've been visiting galleries for fifty-odd years, and whenever I go I come away with postcards of pictures that have taken my fancy. As a result, I have some three or four hundred examples. They serve as souvenirs and as teaching aids: I leave them on children's tables in schools (always at least three times the number I need, so that each child has a choice to make in her study) and they inevitably lead to reflection, discussion and truthful writing. But they are nearly all the same size: in one of the shoeboxes in which I store them, and close to each other, are two pictures from London's National Gallery – Seurat's *Bathers at Asnières*, which is two metres by three, and Van Gogh's *Sunflowers*, which is one metre by three quarters of a metre. If I had bought those cards in a shop, and had never entered the gallery, my mind would have lazily assumed that they were more or less the same size. And even though I do know the originals, the postcards serve to distort my mental image of them.

Another disadvantage with reproductions is that, when displayed on walls, they become dustily dreary. Early Picassos suffer worst. The blue gradually succumbs to the daylight of a corridor until it is a watery grey. And familiarity of reproductions breeds . . . if not contempt, indifference. There's a Millais painting in the Walker Art Gallery in Liverpool, *Lorenzo and Isabella*. It depicts the beginning of a Boccaccio story. It's enough here for me to say that the three young men on the left-hand side of the picture are bent on murdering one, or possibly two, of the characters on the right-hand side: a pair of lovers. Alan Bennett tells the dark story (which children cherish) in his *Untold Stories*.

But although this depiction of a tale of wickedness, worthy of any dark post-watershed soap opera (if there is such a thing) has been hung in schools for the best of reasons, it has become mere decoration. Here it is on one wall as I search for the school canteen. Here it is on another in a different school in the canteen itself. Here it is again in a staffroom. The very availability of the picture in reproduction has taken away its power. It has become no more significant than a glass dome on a mantelpiece with a snowstorm inside when you shake it, or a model of the Eiffel Tower bought for a euro on the Left Bank of the Seine, or that tarnished Tutankhamun's head.

In his book *Ways of Seeing*, John Berger points out that when it is made, each piece of art is unique and in all likelihood has an intended relationship with the room where it was first hung; especially, for example, if it was an altarpiece, or a picture commissioned to be a memorial to a lost member of the family. When it is made into millions of post-cards, its meaning breaks up and is diminished by familiarity. Thank goodness for post-cards, books of reproductions and images available with a click on a screen, of course – but be aware of their limitations. Of how they change the very art that they are, on the face of it, intended to celebrate; but from which they make money for someone, and almost always not the artist. They have changed the art into millions of commodities.

The main reason for taking children to a gallery is to see how much they learn there. The evidence is in the expressions on their faces as they walk around: that quality of attention is attainable in classrooms, yes, of course it is . . . but rarely. And then we note the responses in their talk, their play, their writing and (in the case of the children at St Ives) in the making of their own visual images.

Postscript

Some of the children from the visit to the Ipswich Art School Gallery read my notes on their work; also I spoke to them. This is how their second drafts look.

Maggi's Wave

Dribbling sea splashing
Like the eye of a hurricane.
There is the shape of five dancing dolphins,
a young man falling softly
off his red surf board,
white for the splash of the sea
for the man had fallen off again.

Maggi's Wave

This wave is sad. It makes me cry, cry like the day my mum and dad split up. These waves run down like tears on my face, sad tears, sad, sad tears. Tears for the past, the sad past, the lonely past. The past of bad.

Rosie the Rhino

Black and white,
Squinting eyes,
Bulging tummy,
That's Rosie the Rhino!

Soft upper lip,
Pricked ears,
Strong back,
That's Rosie the Rhino!

Skin as rough as a brick wall,
Horn as hard as a rock,
Slow plodding feet,
That's Rosie the Rhino!

But then . . .

She's scraping,
Scraping the ground
Ready to charge!
Rosie, yes Rosie,
    The Rhino.

Transmetropolitan

There are lots of different colours,
Yellows, blues, greens, reds.
I can see graveyards, churches,
Dying people.

It is a freaky picture.
The small children must
Be frightened in the graves.
Skeletons and skulls are everywhere!

Tiny little stairs and bricks around,
Trains, buses and food,
Logos dotted about.
There's a floating boat and a plane.

Transmetropolitan, that's what
It's called, a very strange name!
Very long and if you
Cannot read it . . .

8

The Sainsbury Centre at the University of East Anglia

Both children and artists see things innocently, as if for the first time.

(Sally Festing, *Barbara Hepworth: A Life of Forms*)

When I was eighteen I could draw like Raphael but I have spent the rest of my life trying to draw like a child.

(Attributed to Picasso)

Except ye be converted and become as little children, ye shall not enter into the kingdom of Heaven.

(St Matthew 18:3)

The pieces of writing by my Springfield children that I've included in that last chapter were not so much first drafts as first jottings. They had scribbled away in the Ipswich gallery, thinking, learning and writing almost as if each of those activities is the same as the others, and I wanted their work to appear here as they first wrote it. It's children's writing in all its roughness ... and in all its potential: many a novel, story, poem or play has begun like this in a notebook. Later, in their activity area where we worked every Wednesday afternoon, they went on to work on these notes, and a few of their second drafts appear in the postscript at the end of that chapter.

I decided that, after the trip to the Sainsbury Centre, I would only print second or even third drafts. This time, after they had made first notes as before, I would read what they had written and talk individually with each child about how they might develop their notes. Teach them, in fact. And then I would put the final articles in this book. I was beginning to know the children well now; or at least, I was beginning to know their different ways of attacking a writing task. Some would begin speculatively by making lists; some would think for a few moments and then write down impressions; some would rush at it in the hope or belief, apparently, that the first sentence or line would be unimprovable.

It helped that I have been awed by The Sainsbury Centre at the University of East Anglia for over a quarter of a century. Norman Foster's building was only some five years old when I studied at the university for a part-time MA, and I have visited the collection many times both during my time there and since. But what delighted me especially was finding that, when I took my young son there with one of his friends, they were completely open to an experience to which many adults are closed. One first adult reaction might be that the structure is, in shape, utterly unlike what you might expect an art gallery to look like.

This begs a question, of course. What should an art gallery look like? Most galleries look as they do simply because they were designed and built in times of Georgian grandeur or Victorian civic pride: wide steps lead up to Greek-style pedimented pillars, between and beneath which the visitors pass on their way through massive doors. In contrast, the Sainsbury Centre looks about right for a hangar accommodating two or three small aircraft. All you see in plans of the place in the handsome 1978 catalogue (Sainsbury Centre for Visual Arts, 1978), whether they are views from the air, cross section or long section, are austere straight lines and right angles. No pitched roofs, no curves, no decoration, no bricks. And in its context, it is a beautiful building – a machine, to adapt Le Corbusier's famous phrase, in which to study and learn about art. It provides a contrast with the surroundings – the water of the nearby artificial lake (called, Norfolk-wise, the 'broad'), the reeds, the trees – and it makes you want to look at both the building and the nature more closely, especially if you are young, or open to new experiences, or both.

The collection here was made by Sir Robert and Lady Sainsbury over a period of over forty years and, as Sir Robert wrote in the 1978 catalogue, each piece was chosen and bought because of the excitement it gave him and his wife:

> I am not ashamed to say that my personal reaction to any work of art is mainly sensual, intuition largely taking the place of intellect. Jacob Epstein used to speak of his 'stomach reaction' to works of art and his phrase perhaps best expresses what I myself seek in the first instance.

I had not planned the afternoon well. We only had an hour in the gallery, and could have used two or three easily. We had to move fast, and I had to make a virtue of the lack of time and make the experience as intense as possible. Once again, as I had at the Ipswich gallery, I took the children to one piece near the main door, and pointed out elements in it that they might be interested in, giving them time to look and think between my urgent questions. I noticed something that should not have surprised me, but which always does, something that I have had cause to remark on several times in this book: nothing short of a loud noise could have taken their eyes off the piece while I talked to them.

What follows are second drafts of what the children wrote in school on the day after the visit, from their scribbled notes made at the gallery. The first piece I directed all the children to before I sent them away to explore on their own was *Headland* by John Davies.

John Davies's sculptures are mostly life-size male figures, completely realistic in mode but with bizarre, possibly symbolic (and equally possibly not) additions. Although Davies always depicts his characters on their own, a bleakness about them often reminds me of Vladimir and Estragon in Samuel Beckett's *Waiting for Godot*. The purposeless sadness of Davies's work certainly struck the children. *Headland* depicts a head over a metre tall:

Headland

He stares straight ahead, thinking
only he's hardly thinking things worth thinking.
Melancholy thoughts whizz round his head
that looks like, well, it's in a trance.
I wish I knew what he was thinking.

This child came up with 'melancholy' when I asked her to think of synonyms for her original 'sad'. The repetition of 'thinking' somehow emphasised the apparent banality of the image, and also this writer's desire to know more.

Another child chose to spend time with *Bucketman*. *Bucketman* depicts a bald individual, dressed in trousers and a jacket that seems to be about to fall off his shoulders. He is carrying two buckets: a ridiculous image comes into my head of those stories, probably libels put about by the French revolutionaries, of Marie Antoinette playing milkmaids while the people starved in the streets of Paris. Behind his head is a curved shape, as if to protect it. And on it is what most interested the children: a plum-coloured blob.

Has he got angry and filled buckets with paint
Then chucked them over his head?
Is he real or has he just been made really well?
Is that a black round ball on his head or is it a plum?
Who is he and why is he a messy man?

One of the most treasurable aspects of the collection at the Sainsbury Centre is the range in time that it covers. There's a figure of a hippopotamus captioned as '*circa* 1880 BC Egypt'; one of Degas' dancers is here, made in the second half of the nineteenth century; and John Davies was born in 1946. This is valuable educationally: timescales like this are hard for all of us to understand, but for children who have only lived fractions of a decade, they are close to impossible. I said to these children: this hippo was made nearly two thousand years before the angels sang on the hill outside Bethlehem; roughly two and a half thousand years before the prophet Mohammed was born; approximately at the time when the pharaoh's daughter found Moses in the bulrushes on the banks of the Nile.

As if to emphasise the wide range, the work is arranged in a way that makes a viewer look at and think about, say, a modern painting of a head by Francis Bacon and then turn, almost immediately, to a head that is four hundred, or two or three thousand, years old. Visitors to this gallery for the first time (like these children) have no idea what they might find next. There are no categories here, and walking round you cross boundaries every few seconds: this is no cosy stroll through the history of art. And the collection is broad in another way, because the larger part of it comes from outside Europe. The children moved among work from Sierra Leone, Ivory Coast, Nigeria, Egypt and other African countries; from New Guinea; from North and Central America; from India and China. This was a seriously multicultural experience for them.

This gallery works against those notions that lie like sodden deadweights in some minds, that 'real' art has certain qualities: that it is representational, even photographic; that it depicts objects – a smile, a sunset, a bowl of flowers – which almost every western European would class as beautiful. The gallery broadens conceptions of what art can be. Much of the work makes you wonder what the motivation for the artist was: this hippo, for example. What was it for? Perhaps to delight just such a viewer as this girl:

Figure of a Walking Hippopotamus c. 1800 BC Egypt

The plump hippo walks to the river slowly every time she goes.
She wants a cool drink after all the running she's done.
It is boiling hot where she is, and she wants to see her friends.
As a stone drops on her rounded head, she knows her mates are nearby.
When she looks round to see them, they see her staring eyes.

This writer's long, slingy line suits the hippo's movement. She had written the piece in the gallery as prose, but when I suggested she break the lines, reading it to herself a few times first and feeling where she wanted a line break, she wrote it out like this. Something has told her that short lines would not suit her subject; that her first line, with the added and perfectly chosen adjective 'plump' (far better than 'fat') would help her reader to see in her words the hippo's progress to the water.

Another writer has arranged her lines with care. This time, though, the poem was written out in the gallery much as it appears here, though there was some careful minor revision:

The mysterious hippo looks out of the glass.
      What are you thinking?
Why are you sad?
What are all the green patches on your back?
    You're looking quite miserable.
        Did something happen?

The mysterious hippo thinks out of his world.
  With his small stubby feet he stays really still.
Are you thinking about something really sad?
Why are you staring longingly all day?
  Your eyes are staring at something.
But no one can make out what it is.

The mysterious hippo stares into space.
      What caused this moment?
Why are you upset?
  What are you seeing inside the grey gloomy skin?
      Your legs are so small.
      What happened to you?

You look so full of yourself.
    Are you ready to go
    To begin a fight?
        I don't know.

Often the children, both in the Sainsbury Centre and in the Ipswich art gallery, were moved to write about sadness. This is partly because of the often-made remark that happiness writes white. The children know implicitly that to write about sunny days, metaphorically if not literally, will yield less interesting lines. But more interestingly, it is also evidence of art's ability to go to places in our psyche, or soul, where there is some emotion or some memory that we need to come to terms with. Our writing can be (the remark is attributed to the American poet Robert Frost) 'a temporary stay against confusion'. This next writer seemed much of the time to be a quiet girl, although this was in all likelihood because of her thoughtfulness: she certainly always wrote sensitively in her sessions with me, and seemed to value them highly. Here she is looking at a portrait of a young woman by Rouault:

Petite fille au ruban rouge
Georges Rouault 1934 gouache
(*ruban* = ribbon, hairband)

She is bright and colourful
when the rest of the room
is dull and grey!
She is looking down at her beautiful
and bright shoes
which are matching her red bow.
She has dressed up for her
tenth birthday party.
But she is bored waiting for her guests.
She's thinking, thinking about
the argument she and her
best friend had.
Is she going to come?

'The argument she and her / best friend had' seems to encapsulate a common, difficult aspect of the life of young girls. It is probably unusual that one has had an opportunity to think about it, and then to encapsulate it in words on the page. The Rouault painting has been a far more powerful stimulus than any suggestion from a teacher about 'those times, we've all had them, when we aren't getting on with our best friend . . .'

Several of the girls but, I noticed, none of the boys, were drawn to the cast of Degas' little ballet dancer. Here is a slightly oblique introduction to some vivid writing about her. I take it to be a test of a lesson: have some of its points been carried over into another lesson without my repeating them? Some weeks before, I had read to the group Chaucer's description of the Miller in *The Canterbury Tales*, the first five lines in the original, the rest in my own prose version. I had emphasised the hard consonants 'b' and 'g' that Chaucer uses in lines like 'Ful byg he was of brawn, and eek of bones' ('He was big in muscle and also in bones'). I pointed out that hard consonantal sounds hit hard like punches through this passage: 'brood' (broad), 'thikke knarre' (sturdy bloke), 'breke', 'blake' (black), 'bockeler' (dagger) and so on. (By the way, the children greatly enjoyed Chaucer's imagery, especially the wart on the miller's nose with hairs 'Reed as the brustles of a old sowes erys', and the man able to break down a door 'at a rennying with his heed'. As a profession, we have underestimated children's intelligence by assuming that none of them is ready for poetry that is so essentially comic, vigorous, truthful and, somehow, quintessentially English.) I had suggested that the children should a choose a modern character well known to them – baker, teacher, police officer – and write about that character using appropriate-sounding consonants.

There was a transfer of learning between the Chaucer lesson and this one in the gallery. The first writer, for example, has taken the point about sounds in words that suit the subject, which was the Degas:

Little dancer aged fourteen

As the dance teacher entered
her eyes were fixed on new people.
The dancer's hair tied in a ribbon, pink.
The skirt frilly, greeny-brown,
feet in fourth position,
arms behind her back. Hooked hands.
That's the girl, the dancer,
the teacher's star.

Here is another dancer standing neat and tall:

Ballet dancer by Edward Degas

I like the way
her ballet shoes point
as she delicately glides
across the floor.

I like the way
she sways her dainty fingers
as she changes her position.

I like the way
she has her hair
neatly tied up in a bun.

I like the way
her fairy-like body
keeps her back straight.

I like the way
she points her chin
towards her next move.

This writer, who knows something about ballet, has allowed her imagination to take the little dancer around the practice room. Her knowledge and experience shows in her words: 'delicately . . . dainty . . . back straight . . . towards her next move'. But there is also a transfer from the Chaucer lesson: all the consonants feel right. No doubt soon she will become painfully aware of the strength needed in ballet, and will revise that daintiness.

The last piece is a bronze by Jacob Epstein, *Head of an Infant*, 1902–4. The mistake in 'suckling' – that 'l' – made for a perfect word here, and I left it in. All writers, of whatever age, need little strokes of luck like this from time to time.

He is bald-headed,
got chubby cheeks.
He's got a hollow head
scrunched up ears.
He's suckling his lower lip, bet I did that.
He's got his eyes closed. Good night baby.

9

Where people worship

1 Castle Acre Priory

This broken paradise.

(Student's writing)

The girls – all aged between nine and eleven – are seriously ill. One clutches her jaw in the agonies of toothache or neuralgia – or has she broken it? Another, cheeks blown out like sails in the wind, seems about to vomit at her own feet. Another has tightened her hood around her head to reveal only the centre of her face: narrowed eyes, wrinkled nose, queasy mouth. Another girl needs to protect herself from something other than the elements, something inside herself, some demon: her empty-eyed, slack-jawed expression suggests some mental illness, the kind described in the New Testament as possession by demons. These girls can't expect much healing or comfort from where they are, and if there are any cures available, they'll be painful.

They are standing on a drizzly day in November against what was once a wall of the infirmary of a Norman monastery. It's now a building, like the rest of the complex, sadly exposed to the sky, but still beautiful to anyone with an eye for such things, a feeling for the humanity that felt the need for them and went to such lengths to build them 'to the glory of God'. I had explained what an infirmary is, and talked about the usual things – lack of anaesthetics, the state of medicine and life expectancy in 1100 compared to now – and the girls are acting the roles of sick monks, and someone, I can't remember who, has taken a photograph.

Later the girls in their blue regulation anoraks walk round the cloisters acting monks from nine centuries ago now restored to health. The silence is perfect: the chatter is stilled, the only sound wind moving through bare trees, as wind has moved for centuries in this place, before these children were born, before their parents were born, before this century and the last . . . before the Normans and the Vikings and the Saxons, before this place – that seems so ancient to the children, to their teachers and to me – was even dreamed of. If one should pray in this place, the prayer would meld with the prayers of generations.

And I have suggested that should they choose, the girls might pray in this cloister for someone they're fond of. Or, if they prefer, they might think about him or her, and all the good things they might wish to happen to that person. Or simply think

Castle Acre Priory

purposefully: meditate. Look at what they can see, and let their thoughts about these walls, this path, that sky, take them where they will . . .

They have already looked hard. They have even smelt the old stones. I recite some words from the mass, not to help them pray, but to give something more of the history of this place, for the sense of hearing: *Kyrie eleison, Christe eleison, Kyrie eleison* – Lord have mercy, Christ have mercy, Lord have mercy.

At the beginning of the session, the girls, their teachers and I had assembled in the priory's old barn. Here we had set the tone of the day. First, there were the necessary words about staying safe: sudden dips . . . dangerous walls . . . streams . . . places where you can't go without an adult . . . no running . . . no going where you can't see an adult. The typical modern classroom has been designed with children's safety paramount, but the priory (like the galleries, forest areas, beaches, streets and other places that I visited while writing this book) were not. In part, it is the slight element of risk in such places that makes them so exciting to the children. To be beyond those walls, and yet still with the encouraging, reassuring presence of Miss or Sir. A kind of freedom.

Then: I didn't lecture on the history of the place. Lecturing is out of place on-site. It is what Duncan Allan calls (in Chapter 5) 'a drip feed of heritage'; it's a waste of time and resources compared to experiencing the real thing – the walls, the arches: the primary sources of history. They could research what follows back at school.

Castle Acre Priory in Norfolk is a religious building that dates from the years just after the Norman invasion, though (the guidebook says) parts were altered in the later Middle Ages. It was a Cluniac foundation, which means elaborate decoration: where in another place the sturdy round arches typical of the Romanesque (or Norman) period would be plain, here many are embellished with layer upon layer of beautiful zigzag patterns, and some of the larger ones have similarly decorated arches snugly fitted inside them. The west front is a superb array of such arches, many of them parts of blind arcades, just there to look good for the glory of God.

The monastery had a relatively short life: numbers fell, and by 1350 there were only twenty monks here compared to the thirty-two who had been here at the beginning. Disease to livestock and the Black Death in 1348 and 1349 had brought the place low. The monks' standing in the town deteriorated, probably due to riotous behaviour of one kind or another: according to the guidebook, Edward III had to order the arrest of some who had 'spurned the habit of their order and were vagabonds in England in secular habit'. It is hard not to wonder what roisterousness, what depravity, what licentiousness this rather official phrasing hides. The place fell into ruin after it was closed in 1537 during the period of Henry VIII's dissolution of the monasteries. The part of this about the monks' bad behaviour would add colour and contrast to the girls' work on medieval history back at school, as would the information from the guidebook that 'in about 1390 twenty-six monks were murdered' here. And they would use their computer skills to research further the history of the place.

I didn't deal with all that here. But I said: 'Look around you. Stare at everything you see for a moment or two . . . . Close your eyes, and listen to the place, to the noises you can hear (utter silence, except for light wind) . . . . Open your eyes and look at these walls. What do they look like? What do they remind you of? What do they resemble? Use your sense of smell . . .'. I was trying to get the girls to pay more than the usual attention; to get into the moods that the place provoked in them. This is a collage of sentences they wrote immediately after this talk:

> The walls felt knobbly and crumbly like dog biscuits . . . they looked like snakes' scales . . . like ripped paper . . . like flint arrow heads . . . spear blades . . . like a jumbled-up puzzle . . . broken picture, ripped-up mosaics . . . the walls of the barn reminded me of a vegetable curry, crumbly potatoes, crisps falling out of a packet, crumbly crumbs falling from a biscuit . . . The windows looked like an ace of diamonds but black instead of red . . . . The ruins look like Medusa's hair on a bad day, and the roof of the porch looks like tangled vines. The trees look like weeping sticks and the clouds look like whipped cream. The pouring rain and the growling wind are the cause of the crumbling structure. Decaying teeth and jagged rocks all remind me of this broken paradise. The arches remind me of cats' arched backs and the patterns on the walls look like old coat racks. The steep spiral staircase made me think of an ever-growing flower, and the ceiling of the porch looked like bending train tracks.

The west front of the church was built between 1090 and 1170, but with remodelling from the later Middle Ages. It will inspire awe in any child given five minutes' silence to look at it. I asked these children to examine it for different shapes – could they describe some of them in mathematical terms? There are many examples of parallel lines and of rectangles. I had already explained how Norman (Romanesque) arches are relatively simple – rounded rather than pointed as arches are a century later. I asked the girls to draw two or three adjacent arches, noting that some of the arches had patterns on the inside of them. I asked them to find other patterns, and I asked them to note that sometimes there were arches in a row that didn't lead anywhere: they are called, today, 'blind arcades'. Why, I asked, are they called 'blind'? I asked, and left them to think about it. The prior's house is next to the west front, to the south; and there is his chapel. This is where the windows shaped 'like black diamonds' were.

Looking *through* was one of activities I emphasised as we arrived, because arches and windows frame objects – clouds, ruins, trees, the village church half a mile away – and this makes the children look harder. Imagine, I might have said, looking at a beach with stones and waves as though part of the scene was framed, a child building a sandcastle with her father; imagine looking at children playing on a playground as though one game, someone kicking a ball, someone skipping, was framed; imagine a scene on a town street, a baby has fallen, a mother leans to pick him up, as if it was framed. Imagine all these as though they were like the pictures in a gallery – framed. The arches and the windows here at Castle Abbey are like those frames.

Sometimes, an archway framed another archway, which in turn framed wintry trees and the surrounding, vast, unhilled Norfolk countryside. We walked round the site – round the cloister again, out past the refectory, past the monks' dormitories; along the stream over which, I explained, was the latrine; we found the place where the kitchen and the brewery would have been:

> Through the arches I can see
> acres and acres of fields.
> Through the arches I can see
> monks killing animals
> to cook in the kitchen.
> Through the arches I can see
> the Priory staring at me.
> Through the arches I can see
> monks going to the brewery.
> Through the arches I can see
> big tall pillars.
> Through the arches I can see
> monks baking bread.
> Through the arches I can see
> monks working in the fields.

Somehow, in flat East Anglia, this writing has a suitably Dutch feel: I can imagine the scene depicted in a painting I've already referred to in Chapter 6, *Children's Games* by the elder Brueghel.

After our tour, we collected everyone together in an earth-floored area that had presumably been a storehouse. Still in the magic of the place, but in a homelier part compared to the west front, the children squatted, read their notes and wrote:

> I looked through the bottom archway
> and saw stones, pointed flint stones
> pile up on each other.

I looked through the top archway
and saw clouds moving in a blue sky.
I looked through the archway long ago
and saw monks praying on their knee
singing hymns in Latin
walking slowly and silently in a single file
taking wine up to the first west end.

The priory provided the children with a chance to examine other lives. Schools rightly emphasise this from the beginning; hence that work with reception about 'people who help us' and the like. In this case, the children had an extreme example. They were appalled to hear that the monks rose at 2 am, attended nine services a day, worked in the fields with crops or animals, or in the bakery, or the brewery; that they ate very little meat, and spent much of their time in silence; and that they spent the rest of the time in prayer and meditation.

At the end of the day at Castle Acre, we gathered again in the barn where we had started. I gave the children a simple structure which can be inferred from what they have written.

Once I was a monk and I prayed
but now I don't pray except at school
and that is boring.

Once I was a monk
and I was holy and believed in God
but now I am Abbie
and I like writing and art!

Once I was a monk and I prayed to God and gave my life to him
but now I am Jessie and I like to party and help others.

There were some younger children there on another day, and they wrote vividly. Charlie, for example, was seven years old:

I can see my face in the glittering well.
I can see a plant in the glittering well.
I can see birds flying over the glittering well.
I can see ruins around the glittering well.

Here the repetition, so natural to young writers with nursery rhymes (one hopes) crowding their minds, helped this boy to make a satisfying poem.

There isn't a school in the United Kingdom that isn't within reach of historic buildings. Even in the cities, there are ruins. I still remember being taken by teachers at my London grammar school on one occasion in the 1950s to see the Tower of London, and the cathedrals at Rochester and Canterbury on another. Details from those visits are still in my mind – the ruins of the

Roman walls – while much that took place in the classroom has long since flown away.

A few years ago, I worked with teachers and schoolchildren on consecutive days at the Bishop's Palace next door to Lincoln Cathedral. Again, I still remember the delight on children's faces, especially as they had the garderobe – lavatory – pointed out to them. 'Henry VIII may have gone to the toilet there' said one child, an image struggling in his mind, perhaps, with the image of Holbein's familiar portrait. The teachers were more interested that this was the place where Henry may have met his fifth wife, Catherine Howard.

2 New every morning: a church

> I love worship places
> where the holy pages
> touch the tips of my fingers
> (Student's writing)

Holy Trinity is a tiny church next door to a primary school in a Suffolk Village, Middleton. The setting could not provide a starker contrast to the setting of the London school whose children visited the Boleyn Ground with me in Chapter 4. Central Park has seven hundred pupils, Middleton fifty; Central is surrounded by shops: a Tesco, kebab shops, newsagents, cafés, and that Essex speciality, a pie and mash shop. The village of Middleton has its school, its pub and its church.

I have often used the church and its churchyard (in springtime the home of ewes and lambs) to inspire the children to write. One writer asked me about the walls, made of a mixture of flint and stones, and I told her that it was called 'flushwork'. She clearly liked the word. Here is the first page of her notes, made on-site:

Diamonds glint like cats' eyes   good angel holding a shield to protect from evil

Crows are like soldiers standing
behind battlements to the tower

flushwork spreads across the church like paint
points like needles sewing the air

protect by wildlife and spirits (End)
stains but who cares it's original

old lions roaring
norman arch smell of burnt cookies
cavemen   damp porch fire burning smoke
your sitting on something that did burn down
it's amazing to think about it.

Pulpit

mould crushing wildlife
stones sticking chancel no birds can get in
the angels playing there   memories in here are amazing!
trumpets soothing the dead

rebels came in smashed the heads

roses beautiful to show how much he loved her

. . . and here is what that looked like when she put it into shape:

Diamonds hidden in the windows glint like cat's eyes.
Crows stand like soldiers behind the battlements.
Flushwork spreads across the church like paint.
The windows look like stickers so unrealistic.
Points stick out like needles sewing through the air.
Stains everywhere but who cares it's original.
Old Norman arch makes you think.
Graves hold spirits and keep them safe.
You're sitting in something that burned down not too long ago.
There are cobwebs hanging paint chipping holes appearing it shows how
                                                          old
        the church is.
A smell like fire burning, damp stone, burnt cookies.
There is mould grows like mad underneath statues.
Rebels came in and smashed the heads of angels who are holding shields
        to protect themselves from evil spirits.

Then, uniquely in my experience, she asked to write a third version which turned out
to be shorter than either of the others:

Flushwork spreads across the church like paint.
Points stick out like needles sewing through the air.
Graves hold spirits and keep them safe.
You're sitting in something that burned down not too long ago.

One regret I have about this book is that I never found an opportunity to work with
children in a place of worship of a religion other than Christianity. I had worked in
a Muslim school some years ago, and a poem that a girl wrote stays with me, in a file,
in my mind, and here:

I love worship places
where the holy pages
touch the tips of my fingers

and prayers are being spoken
by the soft voices.
I love worship places
where the Azan has been called
and men get ready to pray
on the patterned carpet.
I love worship places
where I can face the kaba
and pray with the Imam
with sisters
shoulder to shoulder.
I love worship places
where people say
Peace be upon you
and hug
for respect.

10

Two school journeys

Eloise with a worksheet in a castle

There's a castle we visit where Mr Barret talks
battlements, baileys and barbicans.

But when I've done my worksheet and my sketches
down unsafe stairs I find this lonely place,

this earth-floored larder. I breathe deeply in
the stink of centuries. An ancient chef

sweats. Humps sacks of onions, spuds,
turnips and garlic. Thinks of wine and oil

he'll baste over mutton, pork or lamb. I hear
salt Saxon shouts. Alone, I'm history

and history is me. Be still. Be still . . .
Then Mr Barret's calling 'Eloise!' . . .

He asks me about battlements and baileys
and, not this lonely place, this worksheet.

(FS)

1 Drawing mushrooms over the sea wall

Daniel is my son, now thirty years old and, like both his parents, a primary school teacher. There seemed to be, once he was into his late teens, little doubt about which profession he was heading for, and 'calling' for once seemed the right word (as it always has for me). Because he is able to interpret events that took place when he was at primary school in the light of his training and experience as a teacher I thought he could give this book a unique angle, and therefore he is my chief witness on the subject of the school journey. His first nights spent away from his parents (apart from the occasional sleepover when he was very small) were spent on a school journey to

Hunstanton in Norfolk, when he was ten years old. One Sunday morning we talked about it, and I recorded the conversation:

F   What do you remember about the trip to Hunstanton in Year 6?

D   [*emphatically*] Loads! I remember from . . . getting on the coach at school to the end of it really, and things like . . . the fact that it rained most of time we were there. And I remember being in the dormitories quite a lot, probably lots of things that it wasn't intended that we would remember about it . . . things like our parent helper on the trip who was also the coach driver having to sleep in our bedroom because we were messing about.

    One thing I remember really well was one day when it'd rained all day, it had really poured, and this was summertime, and it was past our bedtime and none of us had been out of the hostel. We all went out for a walk with Miss C . . . the snail incident . . . I wrote that poem that won a prize in a W H Smith competition. Because it had been raining, there were loads of snails out.

    [We found the poem later. I've put it at the end of this section, on p 106.]

    . . . and we went out and we walked along the sea front and there was . . . lads with cars playing very loud music, it was drum and bass, I know now. Drum and bass is associated with clubs and ecstasy. We got chalk and we drew mushrooms all over the sea wall, the chalk was on the floor –

F   Why mushrooms?

D   'Cos that's what we drew . . . at the time. Michael MacKay used to draw mushrooms all over his school books, big chunky mushrooms . . . nothing to do with magic mushrooms . . . . Anyway, it must've been pretty late.

F   Can you remember your thoughts on tucking into bed on the first night?

D   Yeah, I remember not wanting to go and brush my teeth, 'cos I just wanted to be in bed. Feeling really nervous about – everything really, I wasn't in a brilliant state about it all really . . . it only lasted, not being in a good state, when I was on my own and I had time to think about it. When I was with Josh or . . . Nathan or any of that lot I was fine and when we were out and about I was fine.

F   What about these things it wasn't meant you would remember? That weren't official as it were.

D   It was a bit . . . slightly *Lord of the Flies*-ish, really, things boys do when they think no-one is looking.

F   What? Ganging up?

D   Not really like that. You see other sides of some boys. Some boys became quite domineering. Not that it – that didn't really happen to anybody. Obviously we weren't with the girls. In the girls' dorm it was very different to how it was in the boys' dorm.

F   Why?

D   That's very hard to say. In the boys' dorm we were very intent on messing about, whereas in the girls' dorm they weren't . . . . They didn't get into trouble like we did, so I suppose it was different. We did, which was why Mr D ended up sleeping in our dorm . . . on the floor . . .

F   You said 'other sides of some boys'. In the plural. 'Sides.' What other sides did you see?

D   Vulnerability. Like Darren. He was a rowdy rough kid from Denton Street, the best footballer in the school. He has a terrible temper, he used to go mad and score own goals, that sort of thing. He wasn't so tough away. He was quiet.

F   What did you assume – then, as a child – were the purposes of the visit?

D   When we got there . . . there was . . . it was in a Youth Hostel in Hunstanton, so we were taken into I suppose some sort of a classroom really . . . and we were told about birds and things, but really, I think, it was, the real learning intention was far more to take us out. It was for the experiences, really, like in a family holiday.

F   Just that? To take you away from your town, from your familiar environment?

D   Yeah. We went to places like Sandringham and we visited working windmills and the Sea Life Centre . . . . But I don't think there was a specific thing that they wanted us to learn from it, really. Whereas now I think, if you went on a trip you'd go with, you'd have your learning intentions very much specified before-hand.

F   What did you do at Sandringham? Did you meet the Queen Mother?

D   No. We just messed about and threw fir cones at each other. I think even then, when I was in Year 6, that they said that the Queen lives here, etc, etc. I remember . . . even then I remember that I didn't care that the Queen lived here . . . I only remember the fir cones. And that was a day . . . I think . . . that was a day we went to a windmill that was still working, still making bread and I bought a loaf of bread to bring back for you and Mum and then . . .

F   Ate it.

D   Ate it. 'Cos it was so fluffy.

F   Well it wouldn't have been so nice if you'd got it back. So you think the purpose was really just to take you out to these places?

D   Yeah, and I suppose to be our first trip away.

F   The trip itself was sufficient reason? Why? From the teachers' point of view? What do you think Miss A's motivations were, putting them at their highest . . .

D   I can't really say . . . [Understandably: stupid question.]

F   I've got this fantastic phrase, very useful phrase, 'soft skills', Duncan Allan used it to me in Tunstall Forest the other day. In the forest the 'hard skills' were carving, they were making bread, they were weaving, they were gathering wood for a fire, they were getting a fire going, making an axe, cooking. Hard skills. 'Soft skills' are perseverance, collaboration, toleration, blah blah blah. Was your trip to do with soft skills?

D   Probably. But how I would do it now, would be, if I were to run a trip like that I would be far more interested in . . . well, I wouldn't go to a Youth Hostel in Hunstanton. There are very few hard skills you can learn in that environment. If I was gonna do it, I'd do it . . . I'd go with far more purpose. Our Year 6s in school, they go to a residential, they go for a week and there's . . . all activities, things to climb and teamwork skills. There's quite a specific agenda that children will learn to trust each other and get on together and make fires and things. If Miss A and Miss B had had more about them then they would have taken us somewhere a bit more purposeful. When I went to high school I found other kids had far more work ethic, they knew what was going to be expected of them at high school – we hadn't had that. That was something to do with the trip. And other things . . .

F   Were any of the children with you at Hunstanton clearly, no not clearly, were they . . . were they having negative times?

D   I think to begin with people were quite quiet, probably me included. And Nathan was quiet, like I said. But mostly, during the days, things were okay. Mr D was a bit rough . . . that was the incident with a parent . . . that was a fairly unpleasant incident . . . but then I think we all came together closer after that anyway.

F   Like together we stand against this person?

D   Yeah.

F   What did you learn about the other adults that you didn't know before? The only adults you knew were your parents, to some extent your grandparents, aunts and uncles. You were living with these people. What did you discover about them? Their personalities?

D   I have to say I remember very little about the adults on the trip. But Miss C who wasn't a Year 6 teacher . . . so she must've chosen to be there, she . . . when she took us out it had rained, it was dull, whatever we were gonna be doing in the afternoon had been cancelled, it had rained all day, it was summer time, but it was getting a bit dark, it must've been pretty late and what I remember about that is the other teachers weren't too keen on her taking us out.

F   Why was that, do you suppose?

D   I can imagine them saying, 'You know what it's like around here . . . it's late . . . .' Well, it was late, and it was past bedtime, and she just made the decision we were gonna go out and it was rain-soaked, the streets were rain-soaked . . .

F   Tell me about it.

D   There was the smell of grass . . . the grey pavements were dark with rain. There was the sound of water running down gutters, and the sound of boys shouting, boys being allowed out, 'Oy!' But it'd stopped raining. But I think the other teachers weren't happy about her taking us out then . . . I suppose that was a certain amount, you know, of adventure from her. That's one of the things I remember about it.

F   Going out at night . . . in a secure situation, which you were really . . . it was a creative thing to do, wasn't it?

D   Because it was something that . . . though she had not thought it through it was just as creative as if she had. We saw a different side to Hunstanton. We were there in the middle of the summer and it was all very touristy and that sort of thing. We saw those boys racing about, families on holiday, people outside pubs. That was the first time I heard the word 'hot-wired'. Glenn said that to me. They were hot-wiring the cars and playing drum and bass. But Miss C knew that going out . . . that it needed to happen, otherwise we wouldn't have slept. And it kept our attention.

F   I have a working hypothesis for this book: 'On leaving the classroom, children, by that fact, increase their potential for learning.' Sounds like an exam question. Discuss.

D   Yes. Because they start to notice things outside of where they are . . . when you change a display they notice things, but when you take them to an environment where everything is new, whether it's going to the toilet or sitting and eating your lunch or you're being shown things which cause you to have a sense of strangeness, and it could also be what is called 'awe and wonder' in some places, like the British Museum, where I took children once. When they go swimming, when they go to the Ipswich Museum, perhaps for the Egyptian things, but they look at the monkeys! Whatever the aim is, they are soaking up information from all over the place. And you're outside the classroom with them, they see *you* in a different light.

F   How?

D   When you're out with children, wherever, on a day trip, a school journey, whatever it is, the authoritarian side diminishes, there's a companion thing you can't have in the classroom, though I try to have it. Someone says, Why is that like that? Or What is that? Or How did he do that? And you can say, I don't know, how can we find out? It's not so much a delivering-the-lesson thing when you're are out and I think it's great . . . though I am more fierce when we are out, if anyone steps into the road I am fierce . . . the discipline is even tighter . . . . And when you are seeing things that are . . . awesome and wonderful . . . they see you seeing things that are . . . awesome and wonderful!

F   They're soaking up from you and from what they are seeing, and they are soaking up things *about* you, but not just about you, but about how you are when you are seeing what they are seeing . . . . What things in the National Curriculum would you be thinking about if you ran a trip like that now?

D   Environments. Comparing this one to your own. What sort of businesses are there, why they are there, it'd probably be geography based. Sustainable development. You'd be looking at how it was in its heyday, how it's changed now. You'd've done some work on other holiday resorts, places in Spain perhaps. And questioning . . .

Even after twenty years, Daniel is emphatic about what he has remembered, and his recollections are, in places, detailed. In his verbatim account, his words throughout provide vivid colours and textures: the snail, the mushrooms, the chalk, the fluffy loaf of bread, the rain-soaked streets, the noise of the water running in the gutters. This vividness, after all this time, suggests how valuable the experience was (and is); and it suggests, by extension, how valuable all school journeys can be. Such adventures, as I will call them, can last forever in the mind, and be recollected at the oddest times and in the oddest places; like now, like here.

Many children reflect intermittently throughout their lives on what the adults on their school trips were like. There is a dark figure here, driver of the bus and enforcer of discipline in the boys' dorm, who in some way caused the boys to 'come together closer'; there are two teachers dismissed as not having had much about them; finally, and more brightly, there is Miss C who instigates that (for a child) late-night walk, which seems to me to have a special happy significance – the only member of staff who emerges with any clarity or much credit (or much charity). The enforcer of discipline of boys is especially out of focus.

We might compare this with our own memories of school journeys as children. I can't, though – I never went on one – and I have to rely on memories of trips I have helped to run or, later, organised and led. I remember stooping in the tiny room on

HMS Victory where Nelson died. And walking over Isambard Kingdom Brunel's Great Eastern. And being sent to Coventry by a group of Year 6 boys because I had taken them up Snowdon while their football team was playing in the FA Cup Final. And walking with an African Caribbean child, Jenny, who didn't like heights (I don't much either) round the walls of Caernarvon Castle, and feeling her hand sweaty in mine, and seeing her go pale beneath her skin. And ringing a child's father at night because we were worried about her coughing, and greeting him at breakfast time (it was croup).

In all this I certainly got to know many of the children better than I would have done at school, and I wonder what they found out about me. If I could locate one of the thousands of children I had taken away, perhaps they would remember some toilet door that wouldn't lock, or the fried breakfasts, or the colours of a friend's pyjamas, rather than seeing the Roman mosaics at Fishbourne, or walking round the battlements at Caernarvon, or seeing the spot where Nelson is supposed to have said 'Kiss me, Hardy'.

School journeys raise one fear: homesickness. You sense it in Daniel's words about not wanting to clean his teeth: bed obviously supplied something necessary, the possibility of sleep in a personal environment that was at least a little bit like home – though not nearly as comfortable, of course, and surrounded by the unfamiliar sounds of other human beings (Daniel is an only child) rather than Ernest Brown, the bear he'd cuddled before sleep for eight years. A year or two later, he went on a school trip to Austria to learn to ski (no question about the aims there). I gave him a notebook and suggested that he should keep a journal. It still makes my heart lurch to record here the only words he wrote. At the top of first page, and written on the first night: 'I want to be at home.' The homesickness faded with each trip. But he still had nightmares just before the second one. Which he told me about. Twenty years later. During that interview.

One reason why children keep pets is because they die, and in so doing prepare them for greater, more heartbreaking deaths. Love of a football team at age six or thereabouts, assuming that team has variable fortunes, inoculates a child against later and more important disappointments. The reading of poems and stories in which writers face up to human realities – especially the darker realities – can be clearly seen as providing a rehearsal for the dark times in our own lives.

'The real learning intention' Daniel suggests 'was far more to take us out.' If this is true, and it is likely to be so, it suggests that the teachers were aware of this. Being away from home in an exciting environment was something worth all the hassle of preparation and worry and risk, and it was not necessary to think much further about it. I have sympathy with this view. The target model for teaching and learning necessarily misses benefits that are difficult to frame in a behavioural objective, and overemphasises those that are easy to frame. For example, an objective like 'The children will identify the following birds to be found in the area during the summer: . . .', which is both entirely laudable and also tickable, may cause teachers to neglect a more problematical success – the advance a child may make in three days and nights in her ability to get on with her peers and her teachers.

And although later Daniel suggests vague aims aren't sufficient (which, of course, they aren't) and tells how he would be quite explicit in terms of objectives, this getting away from home is a vital experience. Apart from anything else, it leaves us with such memories, not just of things seen and heard and smelt and felt and tasted but of the courage required to overcome the initial loneliness. When we are in times of emotional trouble we remember our courage on our first time away from home, or if we do not explicitly remember it, the fact that it happened strengthens us subconsciously. I suppose this comes under the heading of 'soft skills': like so much that is important in education (and life generally, come to that) it is unmeasurable.

But this bit about learning objectives: 'I don't think there was a specific thing that they wanted us to learn . . . .' Daniel, in his own thoughts about how he would run such an experience, is quite specific. This is partly the result of initiatives in education that lead teachers to think that there should never be a moment wasted, and (this goes with it) that there should be no activity that doesn't contribute to learning. But worse – observable, testable learning.

The walk along the sea front, the loud lads, the chalking of mushrooms: this story depends on Miss C 'who wasn't a Year 6 teacher . . . so she must've chosen to be there'. There is something unofficial about her contribution. She seems to have done what she did as a human being, a parent even (though she wasn't a parent): the boys (only boys went with her) need some exercise or they won't sleep.

This is Daniel's poem 'Snail in Hunstanton':

> The snail as innocent
> as the Birmingham Six
> has come out to damp itself in the rain
> and we
> the giants on the school trip
> have walked down to the dark beach
> with anoraks and wellies.
> I am the unlucky one to step on it.
> I look back and see it there dead.
> I feel hot salty tears
> stinging my eyes.
> Carl (one of us) cracks a joke
> about three men
> but all I can think about is the snail.

2 From a school journey log

> I didn't know you could get so high.
>
> (A student in the Lake District)

One headteacher asked all the adults on a school journey to make a log, and to record comments made by the ten- and eleven-year-old children. None of the children had been on a school journey before. In some cases, parents had paid for their child's place in full; some of the places had been subsidised from various sources.

HEADTEACHER I felt envious as I watched them gather round the coach. I've done loads of school journeys, Wales, Dorset, Hampshire. I wished I was going on this one.

JENNY (a parent) We set off for Buttermere. There was a lot of chatter and exuberance and also some pale, subdued faces. Gradually all the children relaxed enough to enjoy the journey. But it was a very hot day and Jeanette (a teacher) became the Lady of the Buckets as she ministered to the sick. The children seem to have mixed ideas about the forthcoming events. The general feeling was that they were on a day trip and that the coach would be turning round soon and heading back to those familiar and comforting places, their roads, those familiar names, Newton Way, Calvin Crescent, Cowper Drive, Gilpin Road. It was unreal for them that they would actually be sleeping with friends hundreds of miles from anyone familiar. 'I was more scared than excited' admitted Gemma. 'Sometimes you want to get away from home but you miss them don't you?' 'Will we get there today or will we have to sleep on the coach?' asked Darren, a boy whose short fuse worried the teachers.

BARBARA (teacher who had led the trip) I had enough faith in him, even though he had knocked other children about . . . I knew he'd be OK. When we arrived the children talked about television. A concert on last night. Home, I suppose, from home.

BULLETIN OUTSIDE THE SCHOOL. ALL WELL, ARRIVED SAFELY. WEATHER SUPERB. LOVE TO ALL. THE LAKES PARTY. WATCH THIS SPACE FOR MORE NEWS.

JENNY (the next evening) I am sitting in the lounge of the hostel on the first floor. It is 9.00 pm, but still broad daylight and amazingly lovely as I glance up and see the green hills and the mountains through the large window. Sheep baa and move around on the other side of the dry stone wall. I am not alone. With me are a dozen or more showered or unshowered children with lowered heads diligently trying to apply themselves to sketches and summaries of the day's events. Some are in nightwear, having been the lucky ones to have made use of the two showers available for females, and the two for males. Some are still sweaty in their dayclothes. Yesterday's soup – an interesting green colour – is referred to as 'asparagus' by my table and 'sheep dip' by Don's. On today's trip round Windermere someone commented, Margaret I think, '£300 just to walk round a field!' On passing a postcard shop Melanie pointed out a view of Windermere: 'Oh Miss, it's just like Selkirk Park!'

Already the bedding used by the hostel has a new name. It consists of a continental quilt, a pillow, and a cotton item which is rather like a sleeping bag lining. The children call them 'hot dogs'. One of the children asked the staff for 'another hot dog' only to be given a what-are-you-talking-about look. Then it dawned on us: 'hot dog' was an invention, evidence of the unofficial creativity of children left alone for a while to live their lives together.

LAKES PARTY ALL WELL. IT'S VERY HOT AND SUNTANS ARE COMING ON. LOVE TO ALL.

DON (teacher) The highlight of the day was seeing a dipper in a stream we crossed. It was jumping in and swimming underwater as they amazingly do, and re-emerging further down the stream. The children with me just wandered on, much to my disgust: they couldn't see it. Then, as I talked to Jenny, I realised they were looking for a fish. We spent ten minutes watching the dipper then. Later I was comforted by the fact that they saw a buzzard on top of Rannerdale Knotts.

JENNY Most of us climbed our first mountain. I was pleasantly surprised at the generous width of the path zigzagging its way up and relieved to find the ascent within our novice capabilities. David (the school caretaker with the group as an experienced walker) carried a rope, a stove and a rucksack. He was most encouraging about distances and timing. We were within schedule. But it was constantly discouraging when the four of us bringing up the rear reached each stopping point as the vanguard set off again. Nevertheless we placed one walking boot in front of another and, panting with effort, open-mouthed, reached the height of 1160 feet. An enormous cheer went up as a stone was placed on the cairn. 'I didn't know' said Allan, one of the boys, 'you could get so high.' David brewed up some tea. Allan said to him, 'Sir, I think your beard grows more quickly in the sun.'

MARTIN (child) After about an hour me and half the people were tired out. My climbing boots were weighing my feet down. When we stopped a second time to have our lunch we had to do some drawing and some writing. I drawed Crummock Lake. I was looking at the view as I jumped on to a ledge. I lost my balance and fell down another little ledge. I wasn't hurt even though David thought I was. About five minutes later we set out for the top. Mrs Peters and the others who couldn't make it stayed behind. When we got to the top we put a stone there. At the top I took a photo. We could see Crummock Water and Buttermere Lake. We stayed at the top for half an hour and then we had to come down. A little way down we stopped for a game of rounders. At about 4.30 we stopped off at Crummock Water. Some people went in paddling but me and some others were doing skimmers. I got the highest, nine. When we stopped at Buttermere Village Miss went into the village and bought everyone an ice lolly. I bought some mint cakes for my brother.

DON Some of the children seemed quite lost up in the mountain: 'Sir, there's no roads, houses, shops, there's nothing here.'

THE LAKES PARTY ARE WELL AND TIRED AFTER A DAY'S CLIMBING. THEY ARE BEHAVING AND LOOKING FORWARD TO SEEING YOU ON FRIDAY.

JENNY All is quiet except for the birds and the sound of water and the odd child forgetting that this is a period of work. Barbara was talking a moment ago about the contrast between this and where the children live: this green airy meadow, and roads with nowhere to play. 'I'm going to take photos of this so no-one forgets this moment.' Margaret who, the teachers tell me, is all kinds of trouble at school, is behaving perfectly, gazing in wonder at everything she sees. A Catholic charity, I'm told, paid for her to come .... We had a ride in an open carriage on a narrow gauge railway, the one that runs from Eskdale to Ravenglass. I had forgotten about the smuts! Neil wrote something down quickly:

> Here comes a train
> racing along
> faster than lightning
> if I'm not wrong.
> It starts to slow down
> into the station.
> Everyone's pushing
> their friend's relation.
> Boarding the train
> with so much speed
> my helpless shouts
> they do not heed . . .

. . . and so on, rhyming madly. I wonder if he's made that up? Or copied it from somewhere.

The field is littered with buttercups and ferns. Flies buzz around the bent heads of the children. The adults walk about them, pencils in hand.

THE LAKES PARTY WISH YOU WERE THERE. WATCH THIS SPACE FOR ESTIMATED TIME OF ARRIVAL TOMORROW.

JENNY Why is Mr Walne (David) whistling down the phone? We wonder. His dog, it turns out, has snaffled his wife's slippers and won't give them back unless Mr Walne tells him to. Otherwise lots of buzz and activity, last minute packing, tracing lost things, odd socks and unclaimed underwear collected hastily together. Less hearty breakfasts being eaten. Travel sickness pills being issued. Suitcases handed to Terry the driver. The predictable group photo, the gradual shuffle to get everyone in. Then the photo of the four members of the hostel staff, all young, good-natured, in touch with the fun and humour of the children. One of them had emerged from the serving hatch the previous evening and squirted a nicely executed rosette in cream on the bald patch of Phil, one of the parents.

THE LAKES PARTY HAVE LEFT: ETA 6.30 PM. WATCH THIS BOARD FOR CHANGES.

JENNY I loved it all. The sheer friendliness of the children, the feeling of being wanted all the time: 'Will you sit with us Miss?' Melanie had put on her cleanest clothes and packed her suitcase perfectly in readiness for seeing her family again. While Sarah couldn't find any clothes even remotely clean. After dressing she threw everything else into her case saying it didn't matter what she wore, her mum and dad would be pleased to see her anyway. I bet she was right too.

109

THE LAKES PARTY WILL BE TWO HOURS LATE BECAUSE OF HOLD-UPS ON THE MOTORWAY. ALL WELL AND IN GREAT SPIRITS.

HEADTEACHER In fact it was three hours. Back at school we made tea for waiting fathers, mothers, brothers, sisters.

BARBARA An empty playground. My mind screaming with the silence. Nobody came to meet Margaret. She didn't want to go home. 'I wish I was still in the Lake District' she said.

Epilogue

The Basic Skills

There are two silver birches in our school.
One's pollarded and hangs like a willow
over a courtyard where children run
between work and play, between morning and afternoon.

You'd imagine the courtyard a pool
and children free to splash there
and shout and fight and innocuously laugh
and play the fool.

Instead, their feet dry,
they sit in classrooms as the day
like a bright green-skirted angel
drifts through light and shadows,

drifts through light and shadows
with aeon-perfect rhythm.
And Sir their neat ingenuous heads fills
with reading schemes, sums and the basic skills.

Four o'Clock Dance

The children leave the building

Alex and Katrina
Adam Unbenham and James
Alison Greengown and Mac

The children leave the building

autumn leaf and leaf and leaf
and smell of burning in the air

and scarlet roses and scarlet roses
and the one silver birch left

and Ford and Citroen and Renault
and Opel and Volvo and old Vauxhall

The children leave the building

There is no dance and no drama
no painting no poem no page of sums
no songs to sing no construction to be constructed
and checked and measured and drawn

or drawn and measured and checked
and constructed

There is no debate no instrumental playing

There is no art no science no religion

The children leave the building

Katrina and Simone and Jeremy and Nathan
and Syreeta and the other Simone and James
and Gareth and Alan and Margaret and Janey
and Simon and Damien and Mark

and I sit and play the piano
and I sit and paint

and yawn

Rose and bulb and rose
and bulb and rose and
bulb

and autumn leaves

John Crystal

John Crystal was the kindest teacher
        I ever had –
More generous than rain on grass
        But many times as sad.

For Johnny Crystal, he could not
        Control his fountain pen

Let alone the boys then changing
        Into gentlemen.

There were a hundred ways that we
        Eclipsed John Crystal's sun:
'What did you do in school today?'
        'We had a bit of fun . . .'

Then one Monday night I walked
        Back for something I'd
Forgotten in the mayhem of
        Skinning Crystal's hide.

Past the headmaster's office and
        Through empty rooms I move.
They're quiet as the time before
        Needle touches groove.

Then, *piano*, comes the sound
        Of the gentlest kind of jazz
From one of the treasured records that,
        I'm sure, my father has.

I nudge the hall door open.
His gown slung on a chair
His head a-sway to silent drums,
        John Crystal's playing there.

His eyes are closed, his tie is loose.
        On the piano stand
His coffee mug and ashtray
        At the beck of his hand.

Now, John Crystal, when I hear
        Brubeck and Desmond play
I think of how we tortured you
        Day after cruel day.

I think of all the times the sun
        Went dim across your world
Because of the gentlemanly wit
        We nobly hurled.

I see your full head swaying
        And your discarded gown
And hear the fractured melody
        Even I couldn't drown.

Booklist

This is a not a formal list of references. That would be out of place in a book that has no scholarly pretensions. The following list is intended

1   to make it clear when I owe a thought, or an expression of a thought, to another writer;

2   to help the reader to follow up some of my points.

Alan Bennett (2005) *Untold Stories* London, Faber and Faber.

John Berger (1972) *Ways of Seeing: Based on the BBC Television Series* London, British Broadcasting Corporation and Penguin.

James Boswell (1906, first published 1791) *The Life of Samuel Johnson LLD* London, Dent Everyman.

Alec Clegg (1966) *The Excitement of Writing* London, Chatto & Windus.

Jonathan Coad and Glyn Coppack (1988) *Castle Acre Castle and Priory* London, English Heritage.

Tony Curtis, ed. (1997) *As the Poet Said* Dublin, Poetry Ireland/Eigse Eireann. From Dennis O'Driscoll's 'Pickings and Choosings' column in *Poetry Ireland Review*.

Sally Festing (1996) *Barbara Hepworth: A Life of Forms* London, Penguin.

Sigmund Freud 'Creative Writers and Day Dreamers' in P E Vernon, ed. (1970) *Creativity: Selected Readings* London, Penguin.

Bill Grant and Paul Harris, eds (1991) *The Grizedale Experience: Sculpture, Arts and Theatre in a Lakeland Forest* Edinburgh, Canongate.

Michael Harrison and Christopher Stuart-Clark (1977) *The New Dragon Book of Verse* Oxford University Press.

Seamus Heaney (1975) *North* London, Faber and Faber.

Seamus Heaney (1991) *Seeing Things* London, Faber and Faber.

Barbara Hepworth (1985) *Barbara Hepworth: A Pictorial Autobiography* London, The Tate Gallery.

Fred Inglis 'Green and Pleasant Land' in *Literary Review* August 2011.

Jean Mathe trans. David MacRae (1980) *Leonardo's Inventions* Geneva, Minerva.

Margaret Morgan, ed. (1988) *Art 4–11: Art in the Early Years of Schooling* Oxford, Blackwell.

Harry Mount (2008) *A Lust for Window Sills: A Lover's Guide to British Buildings from Portcullis to Pebble-dash* London, Abacus.

Mary Newland and Maurice Rubens (1983) *Some Functions of Art in the Primary School* London, ILEA.

Dennis O'Driscoll (2008) *Stepping Stones: Interviews with Seamus Heaney* London, Faber and Faber.

Iona Opie and Peter Opie (1985) *The Singing Game* Oxford University Press.

Oxford Dictionary of Quotations Third Edition, 1979, Oxford University Press.

A E Popham (1996, first published 1946) *The Drawings of Leonardo da Vinci* London, Pimlico.

Craig Raine (1979) *A Martian Sends a Postcard Home* Oxford University Press.

Christopher Ricks, ed. (1999) *The Oxford Book of English Verse* Oxford University Press.

Michael Rosen (1994) *The Penguin Book of Childhood* London, Penguin.

Sainsbury Centre for Visual Arts (1978) *Robert and Lisa Sainsbury Collection* Norwich, University of East Anglia.

Fred Sedgwick (2011) *Here Comes the Poetry Man* London, Salt.

Fred Sedgwick (2011) *Inspiring Children to Read and Write for Pleasure* London, Routledge.

Suffolk County Council (2008) *Unlocking the Potential: Exploring the Archaeology of Suffolk's Aggregate Landscapes: Final Report* prepared by Duncan Allan.

Barbara Tizard and Martin Hughes (1986) *Young Children Learning* London, Fontana.

Barry Venning (2004) *Constable: The Life and Masterworks* New York, Parkstone.

Leonardo da Vinci (1992) *The Anatomy of Man: Drawings from the Collection of Her Majesty Queen Elizabeth II* Houston Museum of Fine Arts.

Gordon Wells (1986) *The Meaning Makers: Children Learning Language and Using Language to Learn* London, Hodder and Stoughton.

Frank Whitehead (1966) *The Disappearing Dais* London, Chatto & Windus.

Roger Whiting (1992) *Leonardo: A Portrait of a Renaissance Man* London, Barrie & Jenkins.

Marion Whybrow (1994) *St Ives 1883–1993: Portrait of an Art Colony* Woodbridge, Suffolk, Antique Collectors' Club.

Index

Adjectives and adverbs, often redundant 8
Aldwickbury School 27–30
Allan, Duncan (and garbology) Ch. 5, 93
Alliteration and assonance 7, 22, 46
Archaeologists 4, 5, Ch. 5
Architecture 33–37, 98–99
Art as a teacher 82
Auden, W H 1
Augustine of Hippo (*Confessions*) 16
Autobiographical writing by children 15–20

Bacon, Francis (artist) 87
Barker, Dale Devereux (artist) Ch. 4, 52
Bax, Arnold (composer) 57
Bealings School, Suffolk 69–73
Beckett, Samuel (*Waiting for Godot*) 86
Bennett, Alan (*The History Boys*) 36, 83
Berger, John (*Ways of Seeing*) 83
Betjeman, John (*First and Last Loves*) 33, 35–36
Blake, William 3
Britten, Benjamin (*Peter Grimes*) 74
Brueghel, Peter (the elder's 'Children's Games') 61, 95
Brunel, Isambard Kingdom 4
Buttermere (Lake District) 107
Byron, Lord 65

Castle Acre Priory, Norfolk 92–97
Causley, Charles 73

Chaucer, Geoffrey (*The Canterbury Tales*) 89–90
Clegg, Alec (*The Excitement of Writing*) 2
Clichés in children's writing 7
Clouds (children writing about them) 23–27
Confessions (writing idea) 16–19
Constable, John 27, 32
Cope, Wendy 6
Coventry Cathedral ('Christ in Glory' by Graham Sutherland) 72
Crummock Water (Lake District) 108
cummings, e.e. ('maggie and milly and molly and may') 67

Dance and children 49
Davies, John 'Headland' 86; 'Bucketman' 87
DfES Publication 1
Degas, Edgar 87, 89–90
Dench, Judi 31
Dickens, Charles 9
Drawing, children 40

'Editing friends' (part of the redrafting process) 7
Egyptian art, ancient 88
Eliot, T S ('Burnt Norton') 71
Epitaphs 34
Epstein, Jacob 86; ('Head of an Infant') 91
Eves, Guy 'Tulip "Stresa" ' 81–82
Exworth, Roy 'Man Swinging a Boy' 81

Fishbourne (Roman mosaics) 4
Foster, Norman (architect of the Sainsbury Centre at the University of East Anglia) 85
Freud, Lucian ('Girl with a White Dog') 52
Freud, Sigmund 69–70
Frost, Robert 89

Galleries 86 (*and see names of individual galleries*)
Graveyards 34–35
Grizedale Forest Sculpture 70

Haiku 62
Hambling, Maggi 74–84; 'April Wave Breaking' 74–77; 'Scallop' 74–75; 'Wave Tunnel' 77–78; 'Wave Curling' 77; 'Rosie the Rhino' 78–79
Hamilton, Clare (artist) 51
Harrison, Michael and Stuart-Clark, Christopher (*The New Dragon Book of Verse*) 67
Hardy, Thomas ('Afterwards') 31, 37
Heaney, Seamus 6, 28, 70
Hepworth, Barbara 43, 69–73, 85
Herbert, George 23
History and primary sources 50–56
Hood, Thomas 73
Hopkins, Gerard 23, 31, 70
Hughes, Martin *see* Tizard and Hughes
Hughes, Ted ('Wind') 61
Hunstanton, Norfolk (a school journey) 100–106

Ipswich Art School (gallery) 73, 83

Jackson, Paul (storyteller) 71
Johns, Edwin Thomas (artist) 73
Johnson, Dr Samuel 23

Lake District 106
Larkin, Philip 'The Trees' 10; 'First
     Sight' 22; 'To the Sea' 57
Le Corbusier, Charles–Edouard 86
Leonardo da Vinci (drawings) 64
Lincoln, the Bishop's Palace 97
Looking 35, 41

Mandelstam, Osip 71
Memory and writing 13–20, 45–46, 58
Mendelssohn, Felix 71
Metaphor and simile 28, 38–39, 59
Middleton Primary School, Suffolk
     97–98
Millais, James Everett ('Lorenzo and
     Isabella') 82
Monasteries 93–97
Monet, Claude ('Waterlily Pond: Green
     Harmony') 71
Mount, Harry (A Taste for Window
     Sills) 3

National Gallery (London) 24, 27, 82
Newland, Mary and Rubens, Maurice
     41
New Wolsey Theatre, Ipswich 49
Notebooks 50
Nutrition 47

Ofsted 31
Opie, Iona and Peter 6
Oxymorons 62

Parmigianino ('Madonna with the Long
     Neck') 31
Personal, social and moral education
     14
Picasso, Pablo (Guernica) 71, 82, 85

Pissarro, Camille 21, 23–24, 32
Platt, Michael, teacher of dance 40
Play and creativity 70
Postcard, art see Reproductions
Primary sources Ch. 5

Questions in teaching writing 74

Radio 4, 31
Rannerdale Knotts (Lake District) 108
Rathje, William (anthropologist) Ch. 5
Recycling 47
Redrafting 5–8, 24–25, 27, 85
Reproductions 82–83
Rhyme in children's writing 6
Ricks, Christopher (The Oxford Book of
     English Verse) 22
Risk assessment forms 3
Room from the past, The (writing idea)
     14–16
Rosen, Michael (The Penguin Book of
     Childhood) 16
Rouault, Georges ('Petite Fille au ruban
     rouge') 89
Royal Shakespeare Company 3

Safety rules and garbology 50
Sainsbury Centre (art gallery at the
     University of East Anglia) 72,
     85–91
Sainsbury, Sir Robert and Lady 86
St Ives, Cornwall 69–71
Sats 31–32, 36, 52
Science 45
Seaside, children learning at, Ch. 6
Senses 1
Seurat, Georges 'Bathers at Asnieres'
     82
Shakespeare, William 57, 71, 73
Silverton Open Air Museum 4
Simile and metaphor 28, 38–39, 46,
     59
Sketchbooks and sketching 50, 64
Skills, hard and soft 53

Slater, Montague (librettist) 74
Special educational needs and special
     needs co–ordinators 9, 11
Springfield Junior School 12, 23–27,
     36, 73–91
Squirrel, Lawrence (artist) 73
Suffolk County Council Archaeology
     Service Ch. 5
Supermarkets, writing and drawing
     in 40–42
Sutherland, Graham ('Christ in Glory' in
     Coventry Cathedral) 72

Tanner, Robin (choosing as a creative
     act) 72
Tattingstone Primary School 41–42
Tennyson, Alfred Lord 7, 22
Thinking 8
Thompson, Denys 2
Tizard, Barbara and Hughes, Martin 11
     (Young Children Learning)
Truth, telling it in writing 5

Van Gogh, Vincent 'Sunflowers' 82
Vermeer, Jan 23
Victoria and Albert Museum 27
Victory, HMS 4

Walker Gallery, Liverpool 82
Wallis, Alfred 69, 71
Wells, Gordon (The Meaning Makers) 11
West Ham Football Club, writing at
     37–40
Whelan, Brian ('Transmetropolitan')
     79, 84
Whitehead, Frank (The Disappearing
     Dais) 2
Whybrow, Marion (Portrait of an Art
     Colony) 69
Winchester Cathedral 4
Windermere (Lake District) 107
Wordsworth, William 'I wandered
     lonely as a cloud' 21–22, 27–29
Writers, talented 12, 23